INTERACTIVE CITATION WORKBOOK FOR
THE BLUEBOOK:
A UNIFORM SYSTEM OF CITATION®

(2018–Pub.3125)

INTERACTIVE CITATION WORKBOOK FOR *THE BLUEBOOK: A UNIFORM SYSTEM OF CITATION*®

2018 Edition

Tracy L. Norton
Associate Professor of Legal Process
Touro Law Center

Interactive Citation Workbook for The Bluebook: A Uniform System of Citation is independent of and not affiliated with *The Bluebook*.

ISBN: 978–1–5221–4988–0

ISSN: 2329-6283 (print)
ISSN: 2329-6291 (online)

Editorial Office
230 Park Ave., 7th Floor, New York, NY 10169 (800) 543-6862
www.lexisnexis.com

MATTHEW BENDER

(2018–Pub.3125)

Table of Contents

Table of Contents

Acknowledgments

It takes a village to create the ICW! The ICW is a year-round writing, editing, and publishing endeavor made possible only by the tremendous support I receive from my family, friends, research assistants, secretaries, and law school. Specifically, I would like to thank Touro Law Center and, of course, my first-year law students.

We are especially indebted to our longest-serving editor, Cristina Gegenschatz, without whose patience, grace, and eagle eyes, the ICW would not be possible.

Foreword

As an author of a text on legal citation, I am often mistaken for someone who cares greatly about citation. The truth is that I don't. Like most students, I find most citation rules unnecessarily detailed. (Italicized vs. non-italicized punctuation? Be serious.) In the more than 25 years since I purchased my first *Bluebook*, I've seen the rules changed and reversed half a dozen times. I've seen attempts to create a better citation system. They all lead to the same place: an extravagant system of overly-detailed rules.

So why write a citation text and create a citation app for students to learn citation if I don't care about it and think some of the rules are plain silly? Two reasons. The first is that, whether I like any one specific system or not, I acknowledge that lawyers do need some uniform system for attributing the sources that we use; I just don't have the class time to devote to citation when analysis and writing are far more critical skills. Thus, this system of self-directed study for my students to learn legal citation. The second reason I've spent 20 years writing citation exercises and scouring the intricacies of *The Bluebook* is that I do care about my students' credibility before supervising attorneys and courts.

My real passion is helping students become formidable advocates for their clients. A formidable advocate uses every tool available to her to persuade a court on behalf of her client. The first step to being a persuasive advocate is to be someone the court can trust to be accurate, careful, diligent, and professional. Citation is one of the easiest ways for a writer to convey to the court that she respects her client, the court, and herself enough to produce excellent professional work. Because judges (or their clerks and interns) use the citations in a document to look up the lawyer's sources and verify the lawyer's claims, poorly-drafted citations will never escape notice. In fact, it's one aspect of a document that stands out, particularly if the document contains a Table of Authorities.

Judges are professional writers, just as much — or even more so — than lawyers. They appreciate the care and attention to detail required to draft precise, correct citations. Lawyers who don't master legal citation and draft excellent citations are missing an opportunity to impress the court and garner the benefit of the doubt when it's needed.

So, yes, it can be tedious to learn legal citation. But I promise you that it will pay off.

Go be excellent.

Tracy Norton
Associate Professor
Touro Law Center

Using The Interactive Citation Workbook

Layout of the Workbook

The ICW contains seventeen citation exercises. Each exercise builds on and reinforces the skills learned in previous exercises. The goal of this learning method is for you to become familiar with the organization and use of *The Bluebook: A Uniform System of Citation* (currently in its Twentieth Edition, which was published in June 2015).*

You need not memorize the citation rules. However, through repeated use, you will probably find that you have memorized the commonly-used rules.

Each ICW chapter consists of explanatory text and a citation exercise. The text will introduce and explain the rules needed for that exercise, demonstrate by example how those rules are used, and give a checklist you can use in drafting your citations for that exercise. Because each exercise builds on previous exercises, you might find each checklist helpful for many of the later exercises as well. The exercises may be completed in the Workbook and turned in, or you may transfer your answers to the Workstation for immediate feedback. Check with your instructor to see which method you should use.

Beginning to Use *The Bluebook*

The Bluebook is divided into several major sections. To help you navigate it more easily, you may want to tab the sections of *The Bluebook* you will use most: Bluepages, Cases, Statutes, Table 1, Table 6, and the Index. Before you begin any ICW exercises, you should read the Introduction to *The Bluebook*. Pay particular attention to the section titled "Structure of *The Bluebook*." Although the index gets only a one-sentence mention at the end of that section, the index can be tremendously helpful to you. If you have a question about drafting a citation, and you have no idea where to start, the index is your best bet. The Twentieth Edition index is color-coded so that references that appear in text are in black; those that appear in examples are in blue.

You'll notice that the numbering of the Bluepages rules corresponds to the main body rules. Therefore, if you need more examples or more explanation for the rules you see in B10, you would look to Rule 10 in the main body.

A Word about Print vs. Electronic Sources

Each year the legal profession moves away from researching dusty volumes in corners of law libraries to paperless research online. Many (if not most) cases, statutes, legislative history documents, and secondary sources that are available in print are also available through electronic databases or on the Internet. Not only have commercial electronic databases such as Lexis Advance and Westlaw become standard tools of the trade at many, if not most, law firms, but also Internet websites hosted by governmental or commercial

---

* Excerpts from *The Bluebook* used with permission of the copyright holders: Columbia Law Review, The Harvard Law Review Association, University of Pennsylvania Law Review, and the Yale Law Journal.

entities have become numerous and easy to use. Rules B18 and 18 walk us through the proper citation forms for the various alternative sources to primary and secondary legal materials. In addition, Rule 18 contains citation forms for resources that were never in print but have become very accessible to the public: blogs, podcasts, and videos, to name a few.

The Bluebook continues to prefer that legal writers cite to traditional printed sources for reasons of broad accessibility, authoritativeness, and permanence. Therefore, Rule 18 requires citations to traditional printed sources when available. However, *The Bluebook* does recognize that sometimes sources will only be found in nonprint sources or will be much easier to access using a nonprint source. Because our ultimate goal is to enable our reader to easily access the source using the information in our citation, Rule 18 allows citation to a digital copy, either as the only citation or as a supplement to a print source citation.

When appropriate, the chapters that follow will include instruction on both print and electronic sources, and those exercises will allow you to practice both print and electronic citations.

Getting the Most from the ICW

The Interactive Citation Workbook and Workstation (both "ICW") will help you learn the citation rules you will use most frequently when you clerk for a law firm or a court and, later, practice law. The ICW does not cover the rules that most practitioners rarely, if ever, use. However, after completing the ICW exercises, you should be comfortable enough with *The Bluebook* as a reference guide that you can find rules you need to cite any authority.

Because the ICW focuses on citation rules used by practitioners of the law, you will use the typeface conventions that practitioners use. These are found in the Bluepages. You will notice that the examples in the main body of *The Bluebook* rarely follow the typeface instructions in the Bluepages. The reason is that *The Bluebook* examples use the typeface conventions for law review citations (Rule 2.1) rather than court documents and legal memoranda. Take a moment now to read B2 on Typeface Conventions.

Here are a few things you will need to know for every citation exercise:

- The Bluepages allow for either <u>underlining</u> or *italicizing* certain parts of a citation. The Workstation, however, will allow you only to italicize.

- Rule B6 tells you when to leave a space between abbreviations and when not to.

- Rule 2.1(f) tells you when punctuation should be italicized.

- The Bluepages allow you to use large and small caps for style, but does not define what this means. Therefore, the Workstation does not encourage their use.

Students are often eager to "jump in" and complete the online exercises, skipping either the workbook text or *The Bluebook* rules. However, because many of the examples in the workbook and *The Bluebook* are similar to the online problems, students often find that reviewing examples is faster than going it alone.

Students who have the most success with the ICW follow these steps:

- Read the rules identified at the beginning of each workbook chapter.

- Read the workbook chapter.

- Complete the exercise with both the workbook and *The Bluebook* at hand.

Using The Interactive Citation Workbook

- Use the ICW hints to find the rule needed to correct incorrect citations (often the ICW problems will be similar to an example found in *The Bluebook*).

Using the New ICW Platform

LEXISNEXIS® INTERACTIVE CITATION
WORKSTATION GUIDE FOR STUDENTS

Efficiently sharpen and test your citation skills and become familiar with the
organization and use of either *The Bluebook: A Uniform System of Citation®*
or *ALWD Guide to Legal Citation.* Your instructor follows your progress as you
complete problems, while ICW builds on and reinforces the skills you learned
in previous exercises.

Accessing ICW

Step 1: Go to www.lexisnexis.com/lawschool
and sign in using your LexisNexis® ID and
password. That will bring you to the LexisNexis®
Law School Home Page.

Step 2: Click on **Go To Lexis Advance®**.

Step 3: At the top left, click on **Lexis Advance®
Research** and the downward facing arrow (v).

Step 4: Choose Lexis® Interactive Citation
Workstation from the pull-down menu.

 LexisNexis®

Assigning Instructors

Step 1a: The very first time you enroll, a Welcome window will pop up. Click on **Go to Settings** to assign your course instructors.

Or Step 1b: If you click **Close, I'll do this later,** you can add your instructors in Settings on your dashboard:

Step 2: On the Settings page, choose Lexis® Interactive Citation Workstation from the menu on the left.

Step 3: Begin typing your instructor's last name, then choose the correct option from the list that appears. Click **Add**, then click **Save Changes** and Close.

Completing an Exercise

1. Complete any or all problems within each exercise or only the ones your instructor has assigned. Your progress is shown on the left side in the progress bar. The default for each problem in ICW is three attempts, but your professor can change this from 1 to 5 attempts.

2. Use the textbox to enter your citation attempt. The textbox also has specific formatting features that include Bold, Italics, Small Caps, the section symbol and the paragraph symbol.

3. After you have entered your attempt in the text box, click on **Submit Answer**.

Submit Answer

4. When you are done with all of the problems you were assigned for an exercise, and you are ready to send your results to your instructor, click on **Complete Exercise**.

Complete Exercise

1. The ICW dashboard provides a snapshot of your progress across all exercises and includes the last access date and time to help you meet assigned deadlines.

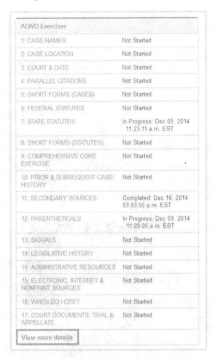

2. Click on **View more details** to see additional information regarding your progress for each exercise, including the number of correct, incorrect or remaining problems you have to complete.

3. You may also review the completion certificate for an individual exercise either in the dashboard view under Actions or in the individual exercise.

4. A link to your completion certificate will be sent to your assigned instructors upon completion (as long as you have assigned instructors in Settings). You may also send to others or download for your files by using the delivery options at the top of the screen. This includes the ability to Save to a Folder, Print, Download or Email the document..

Requesting a Reset

You have several ways to request a reset of a completed exercise. In the individual exercise, there is an option to reset:

Or in the dashboard under **View more details** you can make this request in Actions:

Questions? Send us an email using the student dashboard.

or contact us at **1-800-45-LEXIS**.

Interactive Citation Workstation

It is strongly recommended that students use the Interactive Citation Workbooks to accompany their work on the Interactive Citation Workstation. These workbooks are available for sale on the LexisNexis Store in eBook or print. Students may purchase the workbook via the Dashboard.

Need help?

For additional information about ICW, please click on **More** in the upper-right corner and then click on **Help** in the pull-down menu.

Various topics are covered in this section to help assist you in using ICW...

Chapter 1

CASE NAMES

Before reading the chapter, read the Bluepages introduction, Bluepages rules B2 and B10.1.1, and main body rules 10.1 and 10.2, including the subsections of each rule.

Legal citation, like citation in other disciplines, identifies the source of an idea that a writer uses in his or her writing. A legal citation to a judicial opinion (a "case") has three basic components, all of which are given in the heading of every judicial opinion: the case name, the volume and page number of the source the opinion is printed in (the "reporter"), and a parenthetical that includes the identification of the court that issued the opinion and the date of the opinion. The first three exercises of the ICW will acquaint you with how to use the information given in the heading of an opinion to draft a basic legal citation. When reviewing the examples in the main body of *The Bluebook*, remember that typeface conventions will differ — particularly for case names — for practitioner documents like the ones you are preparing citations for. For example, case names are italicized in the Bluepages but not in the white pages. This is because case names are italicized in the documents like memos and briefs (practitioner documents) but not in law review articles or books (scholarly works). Remember that you should follow the typeface conventions in the Bluepages for practitioner documents when doing the ICW exercises.

The "formula" for a basic legal citation follows:

Party 1 v. Party 2, Vol. Reporter Pg. (Court Date).

The Bluebook quick reference for a case name in a citation is B10.1 of the Bluepages.

A. USING TYPEFACE

The first part of a citation is the case name (*Party 1 v. Party 2*). The case name is made up of the names of the parties. Looking at the citation formula above, you will notice that the case name (*Party 1 v. Party 2*) is italicized. This follows B10.1 and B2 of the Bluepages, which allows for either *italicizing* or underlining the entire case name. When you type your citations in the ICW, you will use italics. Otherwise, you should check with your instructor or supervising attorney for his or her preference. What you might not notice at first glance is that the comma following the case name is *not* italicized. This follows the B10.1.1 Bluepages tip, which tells you not to italicize punctuation when it *follows* italicized material. Italicize punctuation only if it is *within* the italicized material.

B. SHORTENING PARTY INFORMATION

The party information is given at the beginning of a court opinion in the heading. You should list parties in the order they are given in the heading, regardless of procedural posture (*e.g.*, if the defendant is listed first in the heading, list him or her first in the citation). Because cases may involve multiple parties, one or more of which may have a lengthy name, *The Bluebook* provides a system of rules for shortening the case name so that the citation to an opinion is not cumbersome yet still sufficiently identifies the primary parties. These rules are found in 10.2.1 and 10.2.2 with some additional guidance on abbreviations coming from Table 6 (T6) and Table 10 (T10) in the blue pages at the back of *The Bluebook*.

Your citations will appear in either a citation sentence or a textual sentence. A citation sentence is a citation that follows a proposition and stands on its own.

> False imprisonment is the willful detention of another without that person's consent and without the authority of law. ***Employer v. Employee***, 123 **Rptr.** 456 (**Ct.** 2000).

A textual sentence is the proposition itself and may include a citation within it.

> In ***Employer v. Employee***, 123 **Rptr.** 456 (**Ct.** 2000), the court held that false imprisonment is the willful detention of another without that person's consent and without the authority of law.

Rules 10.2.1 and 10.2.2 fall into two general categories: rules calling for omissions and rules calling for abbreviations. The rules for abbreviation differ slightly for citation sentences than those for textual sentences.

The citation rules of omission apply to case names in both citation and textual sentences. However, the citation rules of abbreviation apply primarily to case names in citation sentences. In a textual sentence, the case name is abbreviated according to only Rule 10.2.1(c) without regard to the abbreviations listed in T6 and T10.

Read the rules of omission and abbreviation in 10.2.1 and 10.2.2 carefully before attempting the Case Names exercise. Study the examples to help you understand the rules.

You **should omit** the following general types of information from the citation:

- any actions other than the first in a consolidated case (10.2.1(a))
- any parties other than the first listed on each side (10.2.1(a))
- phrases indicating multiple parties (10.2.1(a))
- procedural phrases (10.2.1(b))
- the word "The" when it is the first word of a party name (10.2.1(d))
- descriptive terms that describe a party already identified by name (10.2.1(e))

- "State of," "Commonwealth of," and "People of," unless the party name is the same as the state the opinion is from. In that case, use only "State," "Commonwealth," or "People" (10.2.1(f))[1]
- "City of" unless it begins a party name (10.2.1(f))
- prepositional phrases of location not following "City," or like expressions (10.2.1(f))
- "of America" after "United States" (10.2.1(f))
- given names or initials of *individuals* unless they are part of a business name (10.2.1(g))
- "Inc.," "Ltd.," "L.L.C.," "N.A.," "F.S.B.," and similar terms if other words in the name *clearly* indicate that the party is a business (10.2.1(h))
- "of Internal Revenue" from "Commissioner of Internal Revenue" (10.2.1(j))

You **should abbreviate** words in a citation in the following circumstances:

- "versus" is abbreviated to "v."
- when the word is listed in 10.2.1(c) or T6 (10.2.1(c) and 10.2.2)
- when the word is a state, country, or other geographical unit listed in T10 unless the unit is a named party (10.2.2)
- when the word is listed in 10.2.1(c) if your citation is in *either* a citation or textual sentence

You **may abbreviate** words in a citation sentence in the following circumstances:

- when the word is eight letters or more if (i) the abbreviation would save substantial space, and (ii) the abbreviation would clearly refer to the party named (10.2.2)[2]
- when the full name of a party can be abbreviated to widely recognized initials (10.2.1(c)). In that case, you would not include periods in the abbreviation according to 6.1(b)

You **should not abbreviate** the following:

- states, countries, and other geographical units listed in T10 and named as parties (10.2.2)
- "United States" (10.2.2)
- any word not listed in 10.2.1(c) *if the citation is in a **textual** sentence*

---

[1] When the government entity is referred to as "The People of the State of" or "The Commonwealth of the People of the," the appropriate abbreviations are "People" and "Commonwealth" respectively.

[2] When doing the online ICW exercises, only abbreviate words listed in T6 unless directed otherwise by the exercise instructions.

When drafting a case name, first omit the necessary information and then abbreviate the rest. Let's try an example of a case name in a citation sentence and then in a textual sentence before you tackle the Case Names exercise.

> Southwest Engineering Company and John Doe, Defendants-Appellants, versus The United States of America, Plaintiff-Appellee

First, let's **omit** all information that the rules require. Rule 10.2.1(a) requires that we omit all parties other than the first, so we will omit "and John Doe" from the first party:

> Southwest Engineering Company ~~and John Doe~~, Defendants-Appellants, versus The United States of America, Plaintiff-Appellee

Rule 10.2.1(e) requires that we omit descriptive terms for named parties, so we will delete "Defendants-Appellants" and "Plaintiff-Appellee":

> Southwest Engineering Company ~~and John Doe, Defendants-Appellants~~, versus The United States of America~~, Plaintiff-Appellee~~

Rule 10.2.1(d) requires that we omit "The" when it is the first word of a party name, so we will omit it from "The United States of America":

> Southwest Engineering Company ~~and John Doe, Defendants-Appellants~~, versus ~~The~~ United States of America~~, Plaintiff-Appellee~~

Rule 10.2.1(f) requires that we omit "of America" after "United States":

> Southwest Engineering Company ~~and John Doe, Defendants-Appellants~~, versus ~~The~~ United States ~~of America, Plaintiff-Appellee~~

Now that we have omitted all of the words *The Bluebook* requires, let's **abbreviate** what's left. First, we abbreviate "versus" to "v." following the examples in *The Bluebook*:

> Southwest Engineering Company ~~and John Doe, Defendants-Appellants~~, v. ~~The~~ United States ~~of America, Plaintiff-Appellee~~

Then, we look in T6 to see which words in "Southwest Engineering Company" should be abbreviated. Notice that T6 abbreviates "Southwest" as "Sw." Next, we notice that both "Engineering" and "Company" are listed in T6; so we abbreviate those words:

> Sw. Eng'g Co. ~~and John Doe, Defendants-Appellants~~, v. ~~The~~ United States ~~of America, Plaintiff-Appellee~~

Finally, we know that Rule 10.2.2 says not to abbreviate "United States." So, all we have to do is italicize the case name, and it's ready to take its place in a citation sentence!

> *Sw. Eng'g Co. v. United States*

But what if we wanted to use this case name in a *textual* sentence? Rule 10.2.1(c) tells us that, in a textual sentence, we only abbreviate the words in a case name that are listed in 10.2.1(c) regardless of whether the words are listed in T6. Neither

"Southwest" nor "Engineering" is on the 10.2.1(c) "short list." However, "Company" is. Therefore, if we wanted to use this case name in a textual sentence, it would look like this:

Southwest Engineering Co. v. United States

Checklist for Case Names

- Have you italicized the case name?
- Have you omitted all words required by 10.2.1?
  - additional parties or actions (10.2.1(a))
  - procedural phrases (10.2.1(b))
  - "The" (10.2.1(d))
  - descriptive terms (10.2.1(e))
  - geographical terms (10.2.1(f)) except when part of a business name
  - given names or initials of individuals (10.2.1(g))
  - business firm designations if other words indicate a business (10.2.1(h))
- Have you abbreviated as necessary?
  - words in 10.2.1(c)
  - words in T6
  - words in T10 unless the unit is a named party
  - party names usually referred to by commonly-known initials (10.2.1(c))
- Have you *not* abbreviated as necessary?
  - geographical units named as parties
  - "United States"
  - all words other than those in 10.2.1(c) if your citation is in a textual rather than citation sentence

Exercise 1
CASE NAMES

Put the following case name information in correct *Bluebook* citation form. All cases are being cited in citation sentences unless the problem indicates otherwise, but do not put a period at the conclusion of your answer because the case name is not a complete citation. This exercise focuses on Rules 10.2.1 and 10.2.2, B2, B10.1.1, and T6.

1. Juan C. Bravo versus The United States of America

2. Erie Railroad Company versus Harry J. Tompkins

3. A Supreme Court of Michigan case, The People of Michigan, Plaintiff-Appellant, versus Jack Kevorkian, Defendant-Appellee.

4. In a textual sentence (as distinguished from a citation sentence that follows a textual sentence), cite Gilbert Dreyfuss, et al., Plaintiffs and Appellants, versus Union Bank of California, Inc., Defendant and Respondent.

5. A single court opinion in a consolidated action styled The Food Studio v. Fabiola's, Fabiola's v. The Food Studio

6. In the matter of Shawna U., et al., Alleged to be Permanently Neglected Children

7. Palm Beach County Canvassing Board, Petitioner v. Katherine Harris, Secretary of State of Florida, et al., Respondents

8. National Association for the Advancement of Colored People Legal Defense and Educational Fund, Incorporated, versus The Committee on Offenses Against the Administration of Justice [*Note: The National Association for the Advancement of Colored People is commonly referred to by its initials, NAACP.*]

9. The Estate of Howard Hughes

10. Robert Downey, Jr., Respondent, versus Motor Vehicle Accident Indemnification Corporation, Appellant

11. Michael J. & Sandra M. Lexie v. Morakis Sons Industrial Painting Company, Incorporated

12. Omni Interests, Incorporated, on behalf of JLJ Resources, Incorporated, Appellant, versus The State of Texas, a United States Supreme Court case.

13. In a textual sentence, cite Catherine Hill, Plaintiff-Respondent, versus The New York Hospital Corporation and Joel Fleischman, Defendants-Appellants.

14. Grady Carter, et al., Petitioners, versus Brown & Williamson Tobacco Corporation, as successor by merger to The American Tobacco Company, Respondent

15. Ned L. Siegel, Georgette Sosa Douglas, and Gonzalo Dorta, as Florida registered voters, and Governor George W. Bush and Dick Cheney, as candidates for President and Vice President, versus Theresa LePore, et al., in their official capacities as members of the County Canvassing Boards of Palm Beach, Miami-Dade, Broward, and Volusia Counties, respectively

---

Chapter 2

CASE LOCATION

> Before reading the chapter, read Bluepages rules B6 and B10.1.2 and main body rule 10.3, including all subsections.

Now that you know how to begin your legal case citation with the proper case name, you are ready to tackle the second major part of the citation: the case location information. Currently, the most commonly used location information for a case is the case's location in a reporter. In that case, the citation "formula" is one you are already familiar with:

Party 1 v. Party 2, **Vol. Reporter Pg.** (Court Date)

However, some jurisdictions have adopted location information that references the year of the decision and a number assigned to the case by the court that issued the opinion. That citation format is called "public domain format." Citations using public domain format use this formula:

Party 1 v. Party 2, **Year STATE No.**

You may or may not be able to tell that the comma following the case name in each formula is not italicized. Rule 2.1(f) tells us to italicize commas that are *within* italicized material but not those that *follow* italicized material. Because the comma after a case name follows italicized material, it is not italicized.

A. REPORTERS

A "reporter" is a compilation of judicial opinions, or cases. The compilation may be by jurisdiction (*e.g.*, *Florida Reports*) or by subject matter (*e.g.*, *Education Law Reporter*). A given case will be published in the reporter or reporters for that case's jurisdiction and may also appear in a subject matter reporter that contains other cases with the same topic. Legal citation, however, references only jurisdictional reporters.

Jurisdictional reporters may be either official publications authorized by statutes of the state or federal government or unofficial publications, often by private publishers. Both official and unofficial reporters are printed in series. Generally, reporter publishers will begin a new series rather than allow the volume numbers to exceed three digits. Therefore, after volume 999 of *South Western Reporter*, Second Series, the publisher next published volume 1 of *South Western Reporter*, Third Series.

State court cases are published in both state and regional reporters. State reporters may be official or unofficial and contain cases from only one state. Regional reporters are unofficial reporters published by West Group. These reporters contain state court cases from several states. For example, *Southern Reporter* publishes state court cases from Alabama, Florida, Louisiana, and Mississippi.

Federal cases are published in jurisdictional reporters by level of court. Federal district court cases are published in *Federal Supplement*. Federal courts of appeals cases are published in *Federal Reporter*. United States Supreme Court cases are published in three reporters: *United States Reports* (official), *Supreme Court Reporter* (unofficial), and *Lawyers' Edition* (unofficial).

Rule 10.3.2 tells us that a citation must include a volume designation, the abbreviated name of the reporter, and the page on which the opinion begins in the reporter. Table 1 (T1) of *The Bluebook* is a listing of information for each jurisdiction in the United States. The listing first gives federal information (T1.1) and then state information (T1.3) organized alphabetically by state name. The first information given for each jurisdiction is the names of the courts in that jurisdiction, the names of the reporters for each court, and the abbreviations for those reporters.

Placing the volume designation in the citation is straightforward. The volume number appears on the spine of the reporter, and that number is the first information given in the case location portion of the citation.

Placing the reporter information in the citation requires a little more information. The abbreviation for the reporter is in the appropriate jurisdictional section of T1. Pay special attention to the spacing of the abbreviation. This spacing follows the rules given in B6. Rule B6 tells us to close up adjacent single capitals (*e.g.*, N.Y.). Ordinals (*e.g.*, 1st, 2d, 4th, etc.) are treated as single capitals (*e.g.*, S.W.2d). Longer abbreviations and single capitals adjacent to longer abbreviations should have a space between them (*e.g.*, Ala. ^ App. and F. ^ Supp.).[1] You can combine these spacing rules to handle both adjacent single capitals and longer abbreviations in the same reporter abbreviation (*e.g.*, N.C. ^ Ct. ^ App.).

Finally, the number of the first page that the case appears on in the reporter follows the reporter abbreviation. When you give the reader the initial page number of the case, he or she has the information needed to find the case.

Hunter v. Gatherer, 789 Rptr. 234 (Ct. 2002).

Sometimes, you will also want to direct your reader's attention to specific material within the case. You can do this using a "pinpoint citation." Bluepages B10.1.2 says that you can pinpoint the location of specific information by following the initial page number in the citation with a comma, a space, and the page number containing the specific material. This specific page number is included *in addition to* the initial page number rather than as a substitute for it.

Hunter v. Gatherer, 789 Rptr. 234, 237 (Ct. 2002).

---

[1] The caret symbol (^) in these examples shows the location of the space but would not actually be included in your citation.

If your pinpointed material spans more than one page, B10.1.2 tells you to give the beginning and ending page numbers, separated by a hyphen or dash.

Tree v. Shrub, 789 Rptr. 85, 87–89 (Ct. 2002).

If the page numbers contain more than two digits, you should drop repetitious digits but always retain the last two digits.

Hunter v. Gatherer, 789 Rptr. 234, 237–39 (Ct. 2002).

Let's try an example to see how these rules work together. Say we have a Louisiana case called *Red v. Green*. *Red v. Green* is published in the Second Series of the *Southern Reporter*, volume 999, beginning on page 111. First, we know that the volume number goes first. It follows immediately after the case name, separated by a comma and a single space.

Red v. Green, 999

Next comes the reporter. It has to be abbreviated, so we look under the jurisdiction of the case, "Louisiana," in T1.3 and find that *Southern Reporter* is abbreviated "So." or "So. 2d," depending on whether the case is printed in the First or Second Series. We know that our volume is in the Second Series, so "So. 2d" it is. Now we check Rule B6 to see the proper spacing to use in the abbreviation. "So." is a longer abbreviation, and "2d" is an ordinal considered as a single capital. In that case, B6 tells us to put a space between them.

Red v. Green, 999 So. 2d

In many reporters, the header of each page contains a notation that reads "Cite as:" followed by the volume, reporter abbreviation, and page number of the case. While we can rely on the given volume and page number, be careful about relying on that header for the reporter abbreviation. The spacing in those abbreviations does not always conform to *The Bluebook*. For example, West's *Federal Supplement* headers give "F.Supp." as the appropriate abbreviation. However, Rule B6 requires a space between "F." and "Supp."

Back to our citation: All we lack is the beginning page number of the case. After we add that, the name and reporter elements of our citation are as follows:

Red v. Green, 999 So. 2d 111

If we were citing to specific pages, 115 through 116, for example, in *Red v. Green*, they would follow the first page of the case. Remember, according to B10.1.2, we add the specific pinpoint reference to our citation after the page on which our case begins. Remember that when a pinpoint reference includes a span of pages, the first and last page of the span should be joined with a hyphen or dash. This page span contains repetitious digits (the "11" in 115 and 116), so this will invoke the rule that any repetitious digits except for the last two should be dropped. Therefore, the first "1" would be dropped because it is a repetitious digit. The second "1" would be retained because, even though it is a repetitious digit, it is also one of the last two digits. Then the name and reporter elements of our citation would be this:

Red v. Green, 999 So. 2d 111, 115–16

B. PUBLIC DOMAIN FORMAT

Rule 10.3.3 provides an alternative to reporter citations. This alternative is called "public domain format." Public domain format allows citation to the year of the decision, the state's two-letter postal code, the court's abbreviation from Table 7 (T7) if the court is not the highest court in the state, and the sequential number of the decision as assigned by the court issuing the opinion.

Party 1 v. Party 2, **Year STATE No.**

Although this is the formula adopted by many states and suggested by Rule 10.3.3, individual states may adopt a different public domain format. In that case, we follow that state's local rules for its public domain format.

By statute, South Dakota now requires that its public domain citations use the abbreviation "S.D." rather than the "SD" that *The Bluebook* lists. Therefore, you should use "S.D." in answering any questions relating to public domain citations of South Dakota cases.

When a citation to a regional reporter is available, Rule 10.3.3 requires public domain format *in addition to* a reporter citation. Otherwise, public domain format is used alone, without a reporter citation. Just as when you cite to a reporter, you can pinpoint cite to specific material using public domain format. In that case, the pinpoint is to a paragraph rather than a page. To determine whether a state requires citation using public domain format, consult that jurisdiction's information in T1.

Drafting public domain format is pretty simple. Let's say you want to cite *Orange v. Purple*, a North Dakota case decided in 2009. This was the ninety-sixth case decided in 2009 by the North Dakota Court of Appeals. The case is not included in *North Western Reporter*, the regional reporter that includes North Dakota state cases.

First, we look in T1.3 under "North Dakota" to see if North Dakota has adopted a public domain format. We find that, for cases decided after January 1, 1997, North Dakota has adopted the public domain format suggested by Rule 10.3.3. Therefore, we start with the year of decision:

Orange v. Purple, 2009

Next, we add the two-letter postal code for North Dakota (ND).

Orange v. Purple, 2009 ND

Because this case was not decided by the highest court in the state, we will also need an abbreviation for the court. We turn to T7 and find that the abbreviation for a state "Court of Appeals" is "Ct. App." Because "Ct." and "App." are longer abbreviations under B6, we will place a space between them.

Orange v. Purple, 2009 ND Ct. App.

Finally, we add the sequential number of the decision, 96. Because we do not need any more information to make this citation complete, we can place a period at the end of our citation sentence. Notice that this differs from reporter citations in that reporter citations require a court and date parenthetical before they are complete. (Chapter 3 introduces you to the court and date parenthetical.)

Orange v. Purple, 2009 ND Ct. App. 96.

If you wanted to direct your reader's attention to specific material, you could use a pinpoint. Remember that public domain cites pinpoint information by paragraph rather than by page. Therefore, if the information you wanted to point out is found in the eleventh paragraph of the opinion, you would pinpoint this way:

Orange v. Purple, 2009 ND Ct. App. 96, ¶ 11.

C. ELECTRONIC DATABASE CITATIONS

Before a case is assigned a reporter location, it will be assigned a database identifier for the various legal databases. For jurisdictions that use public domain citation, that database identifier will be identical to the public domain citation. The citation will also include a parenthetical for the court and date as well as the database name. Consult Rule 10.8.1.

Public Domain: *Johnson v. State*, 2015 ND 7.
Lexis: *Johnson v. State*, No. 20140191, 2015 ND 7 (N.D. Feb. 12, 2015) (LEXIS).

When the database identifier is unique to the database, no parenthetical with the database name is included.

Windsor v. United States, No. 12-2335-cv(L), 2012 WL 4937310 (U.S. Oct. 18, 2012).

The identifier includes "WL" so no parenthetical for Westlaw is needed.

Checklist for Print Reporters

- Have you put the volume number first?

- Have you abbreviated the reporter name as shown in T1.1 (federal information) or T1.3 (state information)?

- Have you closed up adjacent single capitals as shown in Rule B6?

- Have you given the first page of the case, even if there is also a pinpoint citation?

- Have you checked to make sure you have not put an extra space anywhere?

Checklist for Public Domain Format (state cases only)

- Have you consulted T1.3 to see if the case's jurisdiction has adopted a public domain format? If it has, continue. If it has not, give a citation to a reporter rather than public domain format.

- Have you put the year of decision first?

- Have you given the state's two-letter postal code?

- If the case is not from the highest court in the state, have you added the abbreviation from T7 for the court? If so, have you closed up adjacent single capitals as shown in Rule B6?

- Have you given the sequential number of the decision?

- If you need to direct your reader to specific material, have you included a pinpoint to the paragraph containing the material?

- Have you placed a period at the end of the citation?

Exercise 2
CASE LOCATION

Put the following case name information and reporter information or public domain information in correct *Bluebook* citation form. Do not put a period at the conclusion of the "citation" you draft if a court and date parenthetical would be needed to complete the citation. All cases are being cited in citation sentences in a brief to be filed with the United States Supreme Court. Although this exercise builds on the rules used in the previous exercise, this exercise focuses on B10.1.2 and Rules 10.3.2, 10.3.3, 3.2, 3.3, and B6. You will also need to refer to T1 for information on reporter abbreviations and public domain format. If no public domain information is given, assume that none is available.

1. Estelle T. Griswold, et al., Appellants, versus The State of Connecticut, a United States Supreme Court case published in volume 410, page 113, of *United States Reports*.

    _____

    _____

2. Irwin Ravin, Petitioner, versus The State of Alaska, Respondent, a Supreme Court of Alaska case published in volume 537, page 494, of *Pacific Reporter*, Second Series. You wish to direct your reader's attention to specific material appearing on page 515.

    _____

    _____

3. Texas Beef Group versus Oprah Winfrey and Harpo Productions, Inc., a United States Court of Appeals case published in volume 212, page 597, of *Federal Reporter*, Third Series.

    _____

    _____

4. It's in the Cards, Incorporated, and Jeff Meneau, Plaintiffs-Appellants, versus Rosario Fuschetto, an individual, d/b/a Triple Play Collectibles, Defendant-Respondent, a Wisconsin Court of Appeals case published in volume 535, page 11, of *North Western Reporter*, Second Series.

    _____

    _____

5. Richard Hoffer, Plaintiff v. InfoSpace.com, Incorporated, and Naveen Jain, Defendants, a United States District Court case published in volume 102, page 556, of *Federal Supplement*, Second Series. You wish to direct your reader's attention to specific material found on page 557 of volume 102.

    _____

    _____

6. Thomas B. Kee versus Big Cheese Restaurant, Incorporated, a Florida District Court of Appeal case published in volume 767, page 1220, of *Southern Reporter*, Second Series.

    _____

    _____

7. Richard J. Singer, Individually and on behalf of all residents, taxpayers, pedestrians, and motor vehicle owners and occupants of the Commonwealth of Pennsylvania, versus William J. Sheppard, a Supreme Court of Pennsylvania case published in volume 346, page 897, of *Atlantic Reporter*, Second Series.

    _____

    _____

8. Sally McCormick, Appellant, versus Kent England, M.D., and Michael Meyers, M.S.W., Defendants, a South Carolina Court of Appeals case published in volume 494, page 431, of *South Eastern Reporter*, Second Series. You wish to direct your reader's attention to specific material on page 435.

    _____

    _____

9. The State of Maine versus Jake M. White, a Maine Supreme Judicial Court opinion issued as the 219th opinion of 2017 on November 28, 2017. Assume that no cite is yet available for *Atlantic Reporter*, Second Series.

    _____

    _____

10. Jennifer Teeter Plaintiff and Appellee, versus Mid-century Insurance Company, Defendant and Appellant, a Supreme Court of Montana opinion issued as the 292d opinion of 2017 on November 28, 2017. Assume that no cite is yet available for *Montana Reports* or *Pacific Reporter*, Third Series. You wish to direct your reader's attention specifically to material that appears in numbered paragraph 7 of the opinion.

    _____

    _____

Chapter 3

COURT & DATE

Before reading the chapter, read Bluepages rules B10.1.3, B10.1.4, and B18.1.2, and main body rules 10.4, 10.5, and 10.8.1. Remember to space reporter and court abbreviations according to B6.

Congratulations! Now that you have mastered two major parts of a basic case citation, case names and case locations, you are ready to learn the third and final portion of a case citation: the parenthetical containing the court deciding the case and the year of that decision. The court and date parenthetical appears immediately following the page information in your case citation. Now that you have constructed a full citation, you should end it with a period. A case citation used as a citation sentence, *i.e.*, not embedded in a textual sentence, should be punctuated as a sentence: Begin with a capital letter and end by placing a period after the court and date parenthetical:

Party 1 v. Party 2, Vol. Reporter Pg. (**Court Date**).

A. COURT INFORMATION

By looking at a case citation, your reader should be able to determine what court decided the case. Generally, Rule B10.1.3 requires that a legal writer indicate both the name of the state and the name of the court of decision in the court and date parenthetical. Therefore, the court of appeals in Minnesota becomes "Minn. Ct. App." However, some exceptions apply. You omit the name of the court if the court is the highest court in the jurisdiction. This rule is consistent with the abbreviations of state supreme courts, *i.e.*, "Tex." and "Mass." In addition, you omit the jurisdiction information for any court if the title of the reporter unambiguously gives that information to the reader. For example, *United States Reports* publishes only cases decided by the United States Supreme Court. Therefore, a cite to a case published in *United States Reports* can refer only to a United States Supreme Court case. Therefore, you would not include additional information in the court and date parenthetical.

Boerne v. Flores, 521 U.S. 507 (1997).

1. State Cases

Some states have official reporters that publish only cases decided by that state's highest court. For those citations, as mentioned above, B10.1.3 and Rule 10.4(b) provide that no additional information in the court and date parenthetical is necessary. For example, *South Dakota Reports* publishes only cases decided by the South Dakota Supreme Court, and the South Dakota Supreme Court is the highest court in the jurisdiction. Therefore, a cite to a case published in *South Dakota Reports* would not include additional information in the court and date parenthetical.

Landrum v. DeBruycker, 90 S.D. 304, 240 N.W.2d 119 (1976).

However, most reporters, particularly regional reporters, publish opinions from several different state courts. In each of those citations, you must include the jurisdiction and the name of the court that decided the case in question. T1.3 lists the abbreviations for each state court. For example, if you have a case from the Montana Supreme Court, you can look in the Montana entry in T1.3 and see that the abbreviation for that court appears in parentheses after the heading "Supreme Court" and only contains jurisdiction information: "Mont." The court information is not necessary because the court is the highest court in the jurisdiction. Because the reporter abbreviation "P.2d" does not indicate the jurisdiction that decided this case, you would include the entire abbreviation in the court and date parenthetical.

State v. Black, 798 P.2d 530 (**Mont.** 1990).

Similarly, the *North Western Reporter* publishes cases decided by the highest and intermediate courts in seven different states. Therefore, if you are citing a Michigan Court of Appeals case and are citing to *North Western Reporter*, you would convey both the jurisdiction and court information to your reader in the court and date parenthetical. You would use the proper abbreviation for the Michigan Court of Appeals that is given in T1.3 in the parentheses following the heading "Court of Appeals": "Mich. Ct. App." Because the court is only an intermediate appellate court, you must include both jurisdiction and court information. (We will discuss when a writer needs to cite to a regional reporter and an official state reporter in connection with Exercise 4, Parallel Citations.)

Rutherford v. Chrysler Motors Corp., 231 N.W.2d 413 (**Mich. Ct. App.** 1975).

But wait, there's more! *The Bluebook* adds another twist in B10.1.3(v) and Rule 10.4(b). Some states publish an official reporter for cases from more than a single court, *e.g.*, from the supreme court and the appellate courts. Other states have special reporters for just intermediate or trial courts. If the name of the reporter tells your reader the name of the state, then you omit the state information from the court and date parenthetical because it's not necessary; however, you still include the court abbreviation in the court and date parenthetical. For example, if you were going to cite to a New Mexico Court of Appeals case that was reported in *New Mexico Reports*, which publishes cases from different courts, but only courts in New Mexico, then you should omit the "N.M." portion of the correct abbreviation "N.M. Ct. App."

State v. Bartlett, 109 N.M. 679, 789 P.2d 627 (**Ct. App.** 1990).

As you might guess, you have citations like the above example only in certain states; this situation occurs only when you have an official state reporter in addition to the regional reporter.

2. Federal Cases

You must designate a court when citing to any federal case other than a Supreme Court case. The *Federal Reporter* publishes cases from each of the federal courts of appeals. The *Federal Supplement* publishes cases from each United States district court. If you have a case reported in the *Federal Reporter*, you can look under "United States Jurisdictions—Federal" in T1.1 and find the heading "Courts of Appeals" or "Jurisdiction-Specific Citation Rules and Style Guides" in BT2.1. You will see in parentheses after that heading that you must tell your reader which court of appeals decided the case by using the proper abbreviation for that court. The parenthetical provides you with an example. The Court of Appeals for the Second Circuit is abbreviated "2d Cir." Using that example and the table at BT2.1 as a guideline, you can formulate the proper abbreviations for each of the circuit courts of appeals: 1st, 2d, 3d, 4th, 5th, 6th, 7th, 8th, 9th, 10th, and 11th. The federal circuit court that sits in the District of Columbia is abbreviated "D.C. Cir."

> *Deus v. Allstate Ins. Co.*, 15 F.3d 506 (**5th Cir.** 1994).

Pay particular attention to cases decided by the Fifth Circuit in 1981 and 1982. The Fifth Circuit split into the Fifth and Eleventh Circuits on October 1, 1981. Rule 10.8.2 will give you guidance on whether you need additional information in your court and date parenthetical to indicate a case decided during the split.

If you have a case reported in the *Federal Supplement*, you should look under the heading "Federal Courts" in the federal jurisdiction section of BT2.1. Using the listings of court rules for each court, you can form the abbreviation for all the U.S. district courts. The abbreviation for a district court is "D." To that you will always add the state in which the court sits (*e.g.* D. **Mass.**). If that state contains more than one federal district, an additional abbreviation is included prior to "D." (*e.g.*, "**S. D. Tex.**" for the Southern District of Texas). Just remember that, according to Rule 6.1(a), adjacent capitals do not have spaces between them (S.D.N.Y.), but you must put a space between capitals and other abbreviations (D. Mass.).

> *Jones v. Clinton*, 57 F. Supp. 2d 719 (**E.D. Ark.** 1999).

Bottom line: Your reader must be able to tell what court in what jurisdiction decided a certain case by looking at the citation. Whatever information the reporter does not give, you must include in the court and date parenthetical.

B. DATE INFORMATION

Your reader also must be able to glean from your citation the date that your case was decided. Please note that the important date is the date the case was *decided*, not the date the case was *argued* or *heard*. For the majority of the cases that you cite, you will know what year the case was decided from reading the heading of the case in a reporter. For these cases, you simply include the year in the court and date parenthetical.

Stein v. Plainwell Cmty. Schs., 822 F.2d 1406 (6th Cir. **1987**).

Again, watch for cases decided by the Fifth Circuit during the 1981 split. Rule 10.8.2 tells us that for cases decided in 1981, you must also include the month along with the year of decision. (Note that T12 provides the proper abbreviations of the months of the year.)

Also, for cases that are not published in a reporter, you will need to include additional information other than the year of decision, according to Rule 18.3.1. For instance, if a case is not reported or is reported in a slip opinion or an electronic database, then you must give the exact date, *i.e.*, month, day, and year, of the decision.

Williams v. State, 2002 WL 243589 (Ark. Feb. 21, 2002).

C. ELECTRONIC SOURCES

Legal research is performed with increasing regularity through only electronic means. Despite this practice, *The Bluebook* expresses a continued preference in rule 18.2.1 for citation to print sources. Therefore, if you have the information available to cite a print source, you should do that. However, if you would like to provide a parallel citation to an electronic source or if you are citing an opinion for which you only have electronic citation information, *The Bluebook* does allow you to cite electronic sources for cases. This occurs primarily in two situations: first, when the case is unreported but available through an electronic database such as Lexis Advance or WestlawNext, and second, when a slip opinion is available on the Internet.

1. Unreported Cases in Electronic Databases

Note that, if you have an unpublished opinion from a state that has adopted public domain citation (as indicated by that state's section in T1.3), then you would use the public domain citation rules you learned in Chapter 2, Case Location. The public domain citation information will assist a reader in retrieving the case electronically on any electronic database and on the court's web site. Therefore, the rules that follow apply only when the state has not adopted public domain citation form.

To cite to a case that is unreported but available through an electronic database, you will consult rules B10.1.4, B18.1.2, and 10.8.1(a). Those rules give you this basic formula for citation:

Party 1 v. Party 2, No. [docket number], [database identifier] (Ct. Specific Date).

Therefore, the citation to a case found on WestlawNext might look like this:

State v. Kempma, No. 71713-8-I, 2015 WL 1033886 (Wash. Ct. App. Mar. 9, 2015).

Short form citations for cases found in electronic sources are addressed in rule 10.9(a)(ii). If you wish to use a pinpoint citation to focus your reader's attention on a particular page, remember that the pages given in the reporter are not as useful on a computer screen. Commercial databases assign pages in a process called "star pagination." A pinpoint to one of these pages would contain the word "at" and then an asterisk and the page number, even in the long form of the citation.

> *Washington v. Werner*, No. 96-8-00197-6, 1998 WL 283537, at *2 (Wash. Ct. App. June 2, 1998).

The unique database identifier is retained in constructing a short form to a case found in an electronic database.

> *Werner*, 1998 WL 283537, at *2.

2. Slip Opinions

If a case is not yet reported but is available as a slip opinion, you would cite that case using rules B10.1.4 and 10.8.1(b). The citation formula requires that you include the case name, docket number, court, and full date, including the month.

> *Party 1 v. Party 2*, No. [docket number] (Ct. Specific Date).

Because a slip opinion may not be readily available to everyone, providing a parallel citation to an Internet source will improve access to the opinion. B18.1.2 allows for this kind of parallel citation by simply appending the URL to the slip opinion citation.

> *Rodriguez v. United States*, No. 13-9972 (April 21, 2015[1]), http://www.supremecourt.gov/opinions/14pdf/13-9972_p8k0.pdf.

A pinpoint citation for a slip opinion should be to the actual page for the print version of the slip opinion. The phrase "slip op. at" will precede the page number.

> *Rodriguez v. United States*, No. 13-9972 slip op. at 3 (April 21, 2015[2]), http://www.supremecourt.gov/opinions/14pdf/13-9972_p8k0.pdf.

The short form for the slip opinion would replace all location information with "slip op." and would always include a pinpoint citation.

> *Rodriguez*, slip op. at 5.

---

[1] Note that no court abbreviation is included here only because this is a Supreme Court decision. Decisions of other courts would require a court abbreviation within this parenthetical, preceding the date.

[2] Note that no court abbreviation is included here only because this is a Supreme Court decision. Decisions of other courts would require a court abbreviation within this parenthetical, preceding the date.

Checklist for Court Information

- Are you citing from a federal reporter, a regional reporter, or a state reporter?

- If a federal reporter, but not *United States Reports*, have you included an abbreviation for the deciding court as shown in BT2.1?

- If a regional reporter, have you included a full abbreviation for the deciding court as shown in T1.3?

- If a state reporter, have you included an abbreviation for the deciding court, as shown in T1.3, but not the abbreviation for the state?

- Have you double-checked the spacing of your abbreviation according to Rule B6?

Checklist for Date Information

- Is your case published in a reporter? If so, have you included the year of decision in your citation?

- If your case is not reported in print, have you included the month, day, and year in your citation?

Exercise 3
COURT & DATE

Put the following information in correct *Bluebook* form. All cases are being cited in citation sentences. Although this exercise builds on the rules used in the previous exercises, this exercise focuses on B10.1.3 and Rules 10.4 and 10.5. You will also need to refer to T1 for information on the reporters containing cases from the appropriate jurisdiction and proper court abbreviations, and any required public domain formats. For each question, you must use the correct typeface given in B2 and the correct spacing given in B6.

1. L.M. Dennis versus Nelson Gary, a case from the Supreme Court of Washington, decided November 30, 1909, and reported at volume 105, page 172, of *Pacific Reporter*.

2. Jacqueline Suzanne Agathe Jagiella, a/k/a Jacqueline Regaux Jagiella, versus Waclav James Constantine Jagiella, a/k/a Waclav J. Jagiella, a case decided by the United States Court of Appeals for the Fifth Circuit, Unit B, on June 11, 1981, and reported at volume 647, page 561, of *Federal Reporter*, Second Series.

3. Robert Shannon versus Union Pacific Railway Company, a case from the Supreme Court of Kansas, decided February 11, 1888, and reported at volume 16, page 836, of *Pacific Reporter*.

4. The Brotherhood of American Yeomen, defendant-appellant, versus Mrs. Mina Graves, plaintiff-appellee, a case decided by the Court of Appeals of Kentucky, which was the highest state court in that state until 1976. This particular case was decided April 29, 1930, and reported at volume 27, page 670, of *South Western Reporter*, Second Series.

5. Food Lion, Incorporated versus United Food and Commercial Workers International Union, et al. and United Steelworkers of America, et al., a case decided by the United States Court of Appeals in the District of Columbia on January 10, 1997, after oral arguments on November 21, 1996. The case is reported at volume 103, page 1007, of *Federal Reporter*, Third Series.

6. Vivienne Rabidue, Plaintiff, versus Osceola Refining Company, Defendant, a case decided by the United States Court of Appeals for the Fifth Circuit on November 13, 1986, and reported at volume 805, page 611, of *Federal Reporter*, Second Series.

---

7. Derrick Jackson, Appellant, versus the State of Texas, Appellee, a case decided by the Texas Court of Criminal Appeals on May 17, 2000, and reported at volume 17, page 664, of *South Western Reporter*, Third Series.

---

8. The United States of America, Plaintiff, versus The Miami University and The Ohio State University, Defendants, and the Chronicle of Higher Education, Intervenor-Defendant, a case decided by the United States District Court for the Southern District of Ohio. This case was decided on March 20, 2000, and is reported at volume 91, page 1132, of *Federal Supplement*, Second Series.

---

9. Rosemary W. Patterson versus Roger W. Patterson, a case decided on May 28, 1937, by the Supreme Court, Appellate Division, of New York. This case is reported at volume 296, page 311, *West's New York Supplement*.

---

10. The State of New Jersey, Plaintiff-Respondent, versus Ronald E. Staten, Defendant-Appellant, a case from the Superior Court of New Jersey, Appellate Division. This case was submitted on December 8, 1999, and decided on January 19, 2000. This case is reported at volume 743, page 365, of *Atlantic Reporter*, Second Series.

---

11. You wish to cite United States v. Brayan Gomez. This is a December 5, 2017, case from the Second Circuit Court of Appeals. Assume that, at this time, the case is not yet published in the *Federal Reporter*, Third Edition. However, it is available on LEXIS. The unique database identifier is 2017 U.S. App. LEXIS 24502. The docket number is 16-181-cr. [*Note: A case that has not yet been published is not the same as an opinion that has been designated "unpublished" by the court.*]

---

12. You want to cite City of Missoula v. Stephen Leuchtman. This is a 2017 case from the Montana Supreme Court issued as the 303rd opinion of the year. This opinion has been designated as "not for publication." The case was decided on December 5, 2017. The State of Montana follows the practice of denoting unpublished opinions with an "N" (for "noncite") rather than a "U."

_____

_____

13. You want to cite Charmaine Hamer, Petitioner, versus Neighborhood Housing Services of Chicago. This is a United States Supreme Court opinion decided on November 3, 2017. The docket number of the case is 16-658. Assume the case has not yet been published in any reporter and you would, therefore, like to cite the slip opinion from the U.S. Supreme Court's website at http://www.supremecourt.gov/opinions/ 17pdf/16-658_p86b.pdf, which shares identical formatting and pagination to the print slip opinions. [*Note: A case that has not yet been published is not the same as an opinion that has been designated "unpublished" by the court.*]

_____

_____

Chapter 4

PARALLEL CITATIONS

Before reading the chapter, read Bluepages rules B10.1.3, and main body rules 10.3.1 and 10.3.3. Remember to space reporter and court abbreviations according to B6.

Note that 10.3.1(b) tells you that parallel citations are not used in ordinary legal memoranda, such as those that you write in your first-year legal writing course. However, you should include parallel citations when the rules call for them in motions and briefs filed with a court.

Now that you have mastered the basic citation, you are ready to add a twist. The first thing we will add is the parallel citation. A parallel citation is one that contains location information for more than one source of the case.

Fence v. Post, 111 St. Rptr. 222, 888 Reg. Rptr. 999 (2001).

The Bluebook quick reference for the parallel citation is in B10.1.3 at the bottom of page 13 in the first printing of the 20th Edition. Read this before continuing with this chapter.

You learned from the previous exercises that some states have their opinions published in their own state reporter as well as the appropriate regional reporter. For example, opinions from the Idaho Supreme Court and the Idaho Court of Appeals are published in both *Idaho Reports* and *Pacific Reporter*. When you cite opinions from such a state *to a court in that state*, and when local rules of citation require it, B10.1.3 and Rule 10.3.1 tell you to give a citation to both the state and regional reporters. Remember also that some states have adopted a public domain format according to Rule 10.3.3 for citations to that state's opinions. When citing to decisions from those states to those states' courts, Rule 10.3.3 requires a citation to both the public domain information and the regional reporter information.

However, if you are citing in a document to be filed with a federal court or a court outside the state in which the case was decided, you will cite to only the regional reporter.

The first decision you have to make is whether you need a parallel citation. If your case is from a federal court, you will not parallel cite. This rule extends to United States Supreme Court cases as well. Even though they are published in *United States*

Reports, Supreme Court Reporter, and *Lawyers'Edition,* T1.1 tells you to cite to only *United States Reports.*

A. STATES NOT REQUIRING PUBLIC DOMAIN FORMAT

If your case is from a state that has its own reporter and you are citing this case in a document to a state court in that state, you will *usually* cite both the state and the regional reporters. You should consult local rules or customs to determine whether you should cite both the state and regional reporters. BT.2 will help you find jurisdiction-specific rules of citation. If you do cite both the state and regional reporters, you will use T1.3 in much the same way you do for any citation.

First, determine the jurisdiction of the case. Next, look up that jurisdiction in T1.3 Table 1 will tell you which reporters to cite and how those reporters are abbreviated. You see from page 11 of *The Bluebook* that the state reporter is listed first in a parallel citation, and the regional reporter should be listed second. Remember that some cases are printed in many different sources besides just state and regional reporters. Some publishers print subject matter reporters, compiling all the opinions in a certain subject area into one reporter. Also, some secondary research sources, such as *American Law Reports* (A.L.R.), publish the full text of opinions related to the articles they publish. Regardless of the number of publications in which your case is published, you will only cite to the reporters listed in T1.3.[1]

The next decision with a parallel citation is whether and how to identify the jurisdiction and name of the court that issued the opinion. Remember that the general rule, according to Rule 10.4(b), is that you include both the state's abbreviation (*e.g.,* N.M.) and the name of the court (*e.g.,* Ct. App.). The abbreviations for the states can be found in T10 or in that state's section of T1.3. The abbreviations for the court can be found in T7 or in that court's subsection within its state section in T1.3. The first exception to 10.4(b)'s general rule is that you need not include the name of the court if the court of decision is the highest court of the state. So if your case is from the highest court in the state, omit the name of the court, and your reader will assume that the case is from the highest court in the state.

> *W. Edmond Salt Water Disposal Ass'n v. Rosecrans,* 226 P.2d 965 (**Okla.** 1950).

The second exception is that you need not include the state abbreviation if it is obvious from the name of the reporter.

> *Lukowsky v. Shalit,* 487 N.Y.S.2d 781 (**App. Div.** 1985).

Remembering these rules might be easier if you know the rationale behind them. The basic rationale behind every citation rule is to keep the citation as short as possible while still conveying all significant information. This is why we include only the state and regional reporter and not every possible source that might publish an opinion. Also

---

[1] Do not be fooled by citations you read in reported cases! For example, opinions published in the West regional reporter system often contain parallel citations to other subject matter reporters published by West. These types of parallel citations do not conform to *The Bluebook* and should not be copied into your own writing.

for the sake of brevity, we assume that the court is the highest court in the state unless the citation tells us otherwise.[2] Likewise, why include the state abbreviation if it is obvious from the name of the reporter? Wait a minute . . . if brevity is so important, then why use a parallel citation at all? The answer is "convenience." Some practitioners and courts will subscribe only to the state reporter, usually because of financial or shelf-space constraints. A parallel citation helps people using only the state reporter from having to resort to a cross-reference index each time they want to look up a case.

Let's try an example to see how these rules work. Suppose you want to cite the Georgia Supreme Court case *Black v. Blue* in a brief you will file with the Georgia Court of Appeals. This is a 1972 case that is reported at volume 321, page 543, of *Georgia Reports*, Georgia's state reporter. This opinion is also reported at volume 76, page 123, of *South Eastern Reporter*, Second Series. *South Eastern Reporter* is the regional reporter that includes Georgia state cases.

Let's get the easy part of the citation out of the way first. We know we can start with the case name:

> *Black v. Blue,*

Now, let's tackle the first decision: whether to include a parallel citation. This is a Georgia case, and we will be citing it to a Georgia court. Because we are citing a Georgia case to a Georgia court, this case meets the first criterion for a parallel citation. The next criterion is whether Georgia local rules actually require a parallel citation. Assume that you have consulted the local rules for Georgia, and those rules indicate the need for a parallel citation to the state and regional reporters.

Because this is a Georgia case, we will go to the section for Georgia in T1.3. Our case is from the Georgia Supreme Court, so we will be using the first part of this section. This section tells us that *Georgia Reports* is the state reporter for Georgia (and we see also that "Ga." is the abbreviation for *Georgia Reports*) and that S.E.2d is the regional reporter for Georgia cases (we see that "S.E.2d" is the abbreviation for *South Eastern Reporter*, Second Series). This section contains the information we'll need for a parallel citation. It tells us that (1) the reporters we should cite to are *Georgia Reports* and *South Eastern Reporter*, (2) the abbreviations for those reporters are Ga. and S.E.2d, and (3) if the opinion is not in S.E.2d, a citation to Ga. will be sufficient.

Remember that we follow the examples in *The Bluebook* and list the state reporter before the regional reporter. Finally, Rule 10.3.1(b) tells us that if we do not need a parallel cite, *i.e.*, we are not citing a Georgia case to a Georgia court, then we would only cite to *South Eastern Reporter*. Whew! Let's put that information to work:

> *Black v. Blue,* 321 Ga. 543, 76 S.E.2d 123

Now, let's tackle our next decision: how and whether to identify the state in the court and date parenthetical. Rule 10.4(b) tells us that we do not name the court (*e.g.*,

---

[2] Did you realize that citation form and legal ethics are intertwined? Opinions from the highest court in the state have greater authority than lower court opinions. If you do not include the abbreviation for a lower court in a citation to a lower court opinion, not only is your citation incorrect, but you may also be representing to the court that your case has greater authority than it does.

Ct. App.) if it is the highest court in the state. In looking at the Georgia section in T1.3, we see that the Supreme Court is the highest court in Georgia. Therefore, we will not need to name the court. Further, because the name of the state is obvious from the name of one of the reporters (Ga.), B10.1.3 (last sentence before the examples on page 11) tells us that we do not include the state abbreviation. So the only information left to include in the citation is the year of the decision, 1972, and a period ends our citation sentence.

> *Black v. Blue*, 321 Ga. 543, 76 S.E.2d 123 (1972).

Got it? Okay, now take a deep breath, and let's try the same citation in a court document filed with a federal court or a state court outside of Georgia (the rules are the same for both). Rule 10.3.1(b) tells you to cite the regional reporter in this situation, so start with the *South Eastern Reporter* information.

> *Black v. Blue*, 76 S.E.2d 123

Next, decide how and whether to identify the court and jurisdiction in the court and date parenthetical. We are still dealing with the highest court in the state, so we still do not include a court name. However, now the jurisdiction is not obvious from the name of the reporter. *South Eastern Reporter* publishes cases from many states. So we will need to include the abbreviation for the state.

> *Black v. Blue*, 76 S.E.2d 123 (Ga.

Finish it off with the year of decision and a period at the end of our citation sentence, and we are done!

> *Black v. Blue*, 76 S.E.2d 123 (Ga. 1972).

B. STATES REQUIRING PUBLIC DOMAIN FORMAT

Remember from Chapter 2 that T1.3 tells us which states require public domain format. So if you look up a state in T1.3 and do not find a notation that the state has adopted public domain format, you should verify this online.

If a state does require public domain format, Rule 10.3.3 requires parallel citation to the public domain information and the regional reporter. However, if you give a parallel citation that includes public domain information, Rule 10.3.3 does not require a court and date parenthetical unless state local rules specifically call for one. The reason for omitting the parenthetical is that the information that would ordinarily be in that parenthetical—state abbreviation, court abbreviation, and year of decision— are all included in public domain format. Therefore, a court and date parenthetical is unnecessary.

Let's run through an example of a parallel citation that includes public domain format. Suppose we want to cite the North Dakota Supreme Court case *Apache Corp. v. MDU Res. Group, Inc.* This is a 1999 opinion that was issued as the 247th case by the court that year. The case is reported at volume 603, page 891 of *North Western Reporter*, Second Series. *North Western Reporter* is the regional reporter that includes North Dakota state cases.

The first decision is whether our citation should include public domain format. To find this out, we check North Dakota's section of T1.3 and find that North Dakota has adopted the public domain format suggested by Rule 10.3.3. Therefore, we follow 10.3.3 and include both the public domain format and a citation to the regional reporter. Let's start with the public domain information. The first piece of information required is the year of decision.

Apache Corp. v. MDU Res. Group, Inc., 1999

Next, we add the two-letter postal code for North Dakota. Because this case is from the highest court in the state, we do not include an abbreviation for the court name.

Apache Corp. v. MDU Res. Group, Inc., 1999 ND

Finally, we add the sequential number of the case that was assigned by the court.

Apache Corp. v. MDU Res. Group, Inc., 1999 ND 247

Now, let's add the citation for the regional reporter. We find the abbreviation for *North Western Reporter*, Second Series (N.W.2d), in the North Dakota section of T1.3. Because the reporter abbreviation contains only adjacent single capitals, Rule B6 tells us to close up all letters in the abbreviation.

Apache Corp. v. MDU Res. Group, Inc., 1999 ND 247, 603 N.W.2d 891

Because citations using the public domain format in Rule 10.3.3 do not require a court and date parenthetical, all we have to do is add a period to our citation sentence, and we're done!

Apache Corp. v. MDU Res. Group, Inc., 1999 ND 247, 603 N.W.2d 891.

Checklist for Parallel Citations

- Are you citing a federal case?
  - If so, the rules for parallel citation do not apply.
- Are you citing the case in an ordinary legal memorandum?
  - If so, the rules for parallel citation do not apply.
- Are you citing a state case in a document to be filed with a state court?
  - If so, are you citing the case to a state court in that same state (e.g., citing a New York case to a New York court)?
    - If so, the rules for parallel citation do apply. Otherwise, they do not.
    - If so, turn to that state's section of T1.3 to determine whether that state has adopted public domain format.
- If the state has **not** adopted public domain format . . .
  - have you used T1.3 to determine which reporters to cite and how to abbreviate them?
  - have you listed state reporter(s) before the regional reporter?
  - have you included a state abbreviation in the court and date parenthetical only if the name of the state is not obvious from the reporter abbreviation?
  - have you included an abbreviation for the court only if the court is not the highest in the state?
- If the state **has** adopted public domain format . . .
  - have you listed the public domain information first?
  - have you included the citation to the regional reporter if one is available?
  - have you omitted the court and date parenthetical?
  - If the state has adopted a public domain format that differs from Rule 10.3.3, have you consulted local rules for the format and information to include?

Exercise 4
PARALLEL CITATIONS

Put the following information in correct *Bluebook* citation form. All cases are being cited in citation sentences. Although this exercise builds on the rules used in previous exercises, this exercise focuses on B10.1.3 and Rule 10.3.1. You will also need to refer to T1 for information on reporters containing cases in the appropriate jurisdiction and any required public domain information. For each question, you must use the correct typeface given in B2 and the correct spacing given in B6.

1. In a brief filed with a United States District Court, you cite the 1977 United States Supreme Court case Hugh Carey, etc., et al., versus Population Services International, et al. The case is reported in volume 431, page 678 of *United States Reports*; in volume 97, page 2010, of *Supreme Court Reporter*; and in volume 52, page 675, of *Lawyers' Edition*, Second Series.

_____

_____

2. In a brief filed with the Maryland Court of Special Appeals, you cite the 2000 Maryland Court of Appeals case Jacqueline Manikhi versus Mass Transit Administration, et al. The case is reported in volume 758, page 95 of *Atlantic Reporter*, Second Series, and in volume 360, page 333, of *Maryland Reports*. Assume that the usual practice in Maryland is to cite to both the state and regional reporters, in that order.

_____

_____

3. In a brief filed with a United States Court of Appeals, you cite the 2000 Supreme Court of Nebraska case State of Nebraska versus Jesse E. Narcisse. The case is reported in volume 260, page 55, of *Nebraska Reports* and in volume 615, page 110, of *North Western Reporter*, Second Series.

_____

_____

4. In a brief filed with a Texas state district court, you cite the 1971 United States Supreme Court case Alton J. Lemon versus David H. Kurtzman, as Superintendent of Public Instruction of the Commonwealth of Pennsylvania. The case is reported in volume 403, page 602, of *United States Reports* and in volume 29, page 745, of *Lawyers' Edition*, Second Series.

_____

_____

5. In a brief filed with the Supreme Court of Illinois, you cite the 1999 Michigan Court of Appeals case Diane and James Zurcher versus Barbara Herveat. The case is reported in volume 238, page 267, of *Michigan Appeals Reports* and in volume 605, page 329, of *North Western Reporter*, Second Series. Assume Illinois has no local rule concerning the citation of out-of-state cases.

6. In a brief filed with the Oregon Supreme Court, you cite the 1995 Oregon Court of Appeals case GPL Treatment, Limited, a corporation, versus Pacific Corporation, a Delaware corporation. The case is reported in volume 894, page 470, of *Pacific Reporter*, Second Series; in volume 133, page 633, of *Oregon Reports*, Court of Appeals; and in volume 26, page 316, of *UCC Reporter Service*, Second Series. Assume that the usual practice in Oregon is to cite both the state and regional reporters, in that order.

7. In a brief filed with a Massachusetts state trial court, you cite the 1999 Massachusetts Supreme Judicial Court case Dennis Connors versus City of Boston. The case is reported in volume 430, page 31, of *Massachusetts Reports*; in volume 714, page 335, of *North Eastern Reporter*, Second Series; and in volume 74, page 761, of *American Law Reports*, Fifth Series. Assume that the usual practice in Massachusetts in to cite both state and regional reporters, in that order.

8. In a brief filed with the United States Court of Appeals for the Second Circuit, you cite the 1996 Supreme Court of Vermont case Barbara and Michael Murray versus St. Michael's College and Donald Sutton. The case is reported in volume 164, page 205, of *Vermont Reports*; in volume 667, page 294, of *Atlantic Reporter*, Second Series; in volume 104, page 1246, of *Education Law Reports*; and in volume 15, page 372, of *IER Cases*.

9. In a brief filed with the South Dakota Supreme Court, you cite the 2000 South Dakota Supreme Court case Thaddeus Openhowski, Plaintiff and Appellee, versus Alex Mahone, Defendant and Appellant. The case is published in volume 612, page 579, of *North Western Reporter*, Second Series. This case was given the sequential number of 76 by the South Dakota Supreme Court.

10. In a brief filed with the Oklahoma Supreme Court, you cite the 1998 Oklahoma Supreme Court case Black Hawk Oil Company versus Natural Gas Corporation. The case is published in volume 969, page 337, of *Pacific Reporter*, Second Series. This case was given the sequential number of 70 by the Oklahoma Supreme Court.

Chapter 5

SHORT FORMS (CASES)

> Before reading the chapter, read Bluepages rules B4 and B10.2 and main body rules 4.1 and 10.9. Remember to space reporter abbreviations according to B6.

Frequently, you will wish to refer to one case several times within a legal memorandum or a court document. Just to prove to you that *The Bluebook* does indeed have a heart, you need only to give the full legal citation for a case the *first* time that you cite to that case. For all subsequent cites to that case, you will use a short form citation, as long as all subsequent cites are within the same general discussion. Citing a case in full after having mentioned the case before will, in fact, confuse your reader. Your reader may think you are introducing a new case into your analysis.

The citation rules you have learned so far have required that you know only what source you are citing. However, the rules for short forms differ in that you must know not only what you are citing but also the context in which it is cited. Which short form you choose depends on the location of the short form in relation to previous citations to that and other sources.

The Bluebook provides two types of short forms to be used for cases in legal memoranda and court documents: "*id.*" and an abbreviated version of the full legal citation. These two types are not interchangeable, but can each be used only in certain instances. (Note that according to Rule 4.2, "*supra*" is not a permissible short form for certain frequently cited authorities, such as cases and statutes.)

Both B10.2 and Rule 4.1 explain the short form "*id.*" in detail and gives good examples.[1] The short form "*id.*" may only be used when you wish to cite to a case that is cited in the *immediately preceding citation*. In other words, no intervening cites to a different authority of any type should appear between the preceding citation to this case and the current citation. However, the preceding citation to the case may be a full citation or a short form citation, even another "*id.*" designation. Note, however, that simply mentioning a case name in a previous sentence will not support an "*id.*"

---

[1] "*Id.*" is an abbreviation for "idem," meaning "the same." In your earlier studies prior to law school, you may have used "ibid.," which is an abbreviation for the latin word "ibidem," which means "the same place." For whatever reason, legal writing has developed using only "*id.*"

citation. In addition, the prior citation need only be to the same case, not to the same page in the same case. If you wish to cite to the same page of the same case, then use only the word "*id.*" If you wish to cite to a different page or pages of the same case, include those page(s) immediately preceded by the word "at." It is not capitalized unless it begins a citation sentence. The period following the abbreviation is italicized, as provided in rule B10.2.

> Prior to being arrested, Mrs. Jones had accumulated over 100 speeding tickets. *State v. Jones*, 16 Rptr. 33, 34 (St. Ct. 1999). The majority of these tickets listed her speed as at least 20 miles per hour over the posted speed limit. *Id.* Five of the speeding tickets were issued in connection with traffic accidents. *Id.* at 35.

One more detail to remember: If the immediately preceding citation is a "string cite," *i.e.*, contains more than one authority, then you may not use "*id.*," even if one of those authorities is the case you currently wish to cite. Consider the following three cites that appear consecutively in a paragraph.

State v. Jones, 16 Rptr. 33, 34 (St. Ct. 1999).

Id.; *State v. Smith*, 19 Rptr. 389, 390-92 (St. Ct. 2002).

Smith, 19 Rptr. at 390-92.

The second citation is a string cite referring to both *Jones* and *Smith*. Because *Jones* was the immediately preceding citation, "*id.*" clearly refers to that case. "*Id.*" may be part of a string cite. However, notice that the third citation, a reference to *Smith*, is not "*id.*" even though *Smith* is part of the immediately preceding citation. This is because "*id.*" cannot be used to refer to a single source within a string cite. When you think about it, this makes sense. If the second citation above were followed by "*id.*" the reader would likely think you intended a citation to both of the sources in the string cite.

When circumstances do not allow you to use "*id.*," you must use an abbreviated form of the full citation. Although Rule 10.9 tells us that in formulating our short form we may use (i) both parties' names, (ii) one party's name, or (iii) neither party's name, B10.2 allows the use of only alternatives (ii) and (iii) in legal memoranda and court documents. In addition, you must retain the volume number of the reporter and the reporter abbreviation. However, you do not include the first page on which your case appears, but instead you give the number of the page on which you wish to focus your reader's attention, preceded by the word "at." You drop the court and date parenthetical completely:

Party, Vol. Reporter at Pg.

or

Vol. Reporter at Pg.

Therefore, if you wanted to formulate a short form to refer to page 33 of the case *Gagnon v. Adamson*, 264 P.2d 31 (Cal. 1953), under B10.2 you would have two options:

Gagnon, 264 P.2d at 33.

or

264 P.2d at 33.

Either of these forms is acceptable, but you may develop your own preference or decide that in certain situations one form is clearer than the other.

Most legal writers choose to include one party's name in an abbreviated short form. In addition, most legal writers choose to refer to a case by the party's name that appears first in the case name, and the new B10.2 reflects this usage by requiring the use of the name of the first party.

However, B10.2 warns you not to use the name of the first party if that party is frequently a party to litigation, such as a state, the United States, a governmental agency, or the head of an agency or branch of government of either a state or the United States. Therefore, for the case *State v. Roach*, 772 A.2d 395 (N.J. 2001), you would choose as your short form.

Roach, 772 A.2d at 400.

NOT:

State, 772 A.2d at 400.

On caution about forming short form citations for your cases. While you have seen that you have some flexibility in how you draft your short form, remember that your reader must be able to find the case using only the short form. Therefore, the short form must include the volume number, reporter abbreviation, and pinpoint page number. Without that information, the reader cannot use the citation to locate the case.

NOT: *Roach* at 400.

If the full citation of your case is a parallel citation with two or more reporter references, then craft your abbreviated short form in accordance with B10.2. Again, you would drop the first page on which your case appears in each reporter and the court and date parenthetical, but include the relevant page information for each reporter preceded by the word "at."

Roach, 167 N.J. at 600, 772 A.2d at 400.

If you are using an electronic print-out of the case, you will use the star-paging to find the pinpoint numbers for each reporter in your citation. Generally, each reporter will have a different number of asterisks assigned to its page numbers in the electronic version of the case. Therefore, all of the regional reporter cites might be accompanied by one asterisk, and all state reporter cites might be accompanied by two. By using the citations at the beginning of the case and a little bit of deductive reasoning, you will easily be able to figure out which page numbers correspond to which reporter so you can include them in your pinpoint citation.

For the use of "*id.*" with a parallel citation, you would include the volume and reporter information of all reporters but the official state reporter, which appears first in your citation.

Id. at 255, 264 P.2d at 33.

Checklist for Case Short Forms

- Did you cite to the current case in the immediately preceding citation? If so, use "*id.*" If not, then you cannot use "*id.*" and must use an abbreviated short form.

- Does the immediately preceding citation contain more than one authority, *i.e.*, is it a string cite? If so, then you cannot use "*id.*" and must use an abbreviated short form.

- If you cannot use "*id.*," have you formulated an acceptable abbreviated short form?

- In your abbreviated short form, have you retained the volume and reporter name from the full legal citation?

- If the full citation contained a parallel citation, have you included references to both reporters in the short form?

- In your abbreviated short form, have you used the word "at" and a pinpoint page number?

Exercise 5
SHORT FORMS (CASES)

Put the following information in correct *Bluebook* citation form. All cases are being cited in citation sentences. Although this exercise builds on the rules used in previous exercises, this exercise focuses on B10.2 and Rules 4.1 and 10.9. Although the Bluepages teach us two alternatives for short forms that are equally acceptable, follow the instructions in each question for formulating short forms. In composing the short form names, be guided by the information in each citation problem. For each question, you must use the correct typeface given in B2 and the correct spacing given in B6.

1. In the immediately preceding sentence of a legal memorandum, without an intervening cite, you cited to *Hanjaras v. City of Atlanta*, 65 S.E. 356 (Ga. Ct. App. 1909). You now wish to cite to page 357 of the case. You have been referring to this case in text as "*Hanjaras*."

2. A few paragraphs later, after citing to other cases and a statute, you wish to cite to page 357 of *Hanjaras v. City of Atlanta*, 65 S.E. 356 (Ga. Ct. App. 1909). You have been referring to this case in text as "*Hanjaras*."

3. On page 2 of your legal memorandum, you cited to *Riner v. State*, 1 So. 2d 402 (Ala. Ct. App. 1941). In the same general discussion on page 4 of your memo, you would like to cite to *Riner* again, only you would like to focus your reader's attention on information beginning on page 402 and continuing on page 403 of the court's opinion. You have cited to other cases on pages 3 and 4 of your memorandum.

4. In the next sentence, you would like to cite again to *Riner v. State*, 1 So. 2d 402 (Ala. Ct. App. 1941), again focusing your reader on information from pages 402 to 403. No intervening cites appear between the citation in Problem 3 and the current cite.

5. In the same legal memorandum, you again wish to refer to *Hanjaras v. City of Atlanta*, 65 S.E. 356 (Ga. Ct. App. 1909), focusing your reader's attention on information on page 357. The immediately preceding citation sentence reads "*Hanjaras*, 65 S.E. at 357; *Riner*, 1 So. 2d at 403."

6. In a brief to a Missouri court, you have previously cited to *State ex rel. Kenamore v. Wood*, 155 Mo. 425, 56 S.W. 474 (1900). You wish to cite to *Kenamore* again after several intervening cites, focusing your reader's attention on information contained at page 475 of *South Western Reporter* and page 426 of *Missouri Reports*.

---

7. In the next sentence, without any intervening cites you would like to cite to *Kenamore* again, only this time you would like to direct your reader's attention to information found at page 476 of *South Western Reporter* and page 427 of *Missouri Reports*. [For your reference, the text of Problem 6 is: In a brief to a Missouri court, you have previously cited to *State ex rel. Kenamore v. Wood*, 155 Mo. 425, 56 S.W. 474 (1900). You wish to cite to *Kenamore* again after several intervening cites, focusing your reader's attention on information contained at page 475 of *South Western Reporter* and page 426 of *Missouri Reports*.]

---

8. On page 16 of a brief to the United States Court of Appeals for the Second Circuit, you cite to *Guinness v. United States*, 73 F. Supp. 119 (Ct. Cl. 1947). In the same general discussion on page 22 of your brief, you would like to refer to this case again, focusing your reader's attention on information beginning on page 120 and continuing on page 121 of the court's opinion. You have cited to other cases in the interim.

---

9. You wish to formulate a short form, not "*id.*," for information found on the first page of *Anheuser-Busch, Inc. v. Comm'r*, 115 F.2d 662 (8th Cir. 1940), a tax case between a Missouri corporation and the Commissioner of Internal Revenue. You have referred to the corporation as "Anheuser-Busch."

---

10. In the very next sentence, without an intervening cite, you wish to formulate a string cite, for information that can be found on page 665 of *Anheuser-Busch, Inc. v. Comm'r*, 115 F.2d 662 (8th Cir. 1940), which you have just cited, and also on page 313 of *Hedden v. Comm'r*, 105 F.2d 311 (3d Cir. 1939), which you have not yet cited.

Chapter 6

FEDERAL STATUTES

Before reading the chapter, read Bluepages rules B11, B12.1.1, B12.1.3, B12.1.4, and main body rules 11, 12.1.-12.3, 12.5, and 12.9.1-12.9.3. Remember to space the statute abbreviation using B6.

The general rules for citing federal statutes are located in Chapter 12 of *The Bluebook*. Be aware, however, that the examples of statutory citations you will see in *The Bluebook* are printed in LARGE AND SMALL CAPITAL LETTERS. The corresponding Bluepages sections, B12.1.1 and B12.1.2, use normal typeface in their examples for statutes and constitutions. Rule B2 does not list statute names as one of the few elements of a citation that should not appear in ordinary roman type. You will remember that the ICW expects (and most legal employers and judges expect) you to use the rules in the Bluepages for legal memoranda and court documents. Therefore, you will use ordinary roman type (upper and lower case letters) rather than large and small capitals.[1] In addition to B12.1.1, you will also need to be familiar with Rules 3.2, 3.4, 6.1, and 6.2 and the federal portion of T1.1. Also, although the United States Constitution is not technically a statute, it is included in this exercise, so you will also use B11 and Rule 11 of *The Bluebook*.

Both the federal statutes and the United States Constitution are published in an official compilation, the *United States Code*. The federal statutes compiled in the *United States Code* are divided into fifty subject matter areas called "titles." Each title is numbered and may span more than one hard-bound volume. Within each title, each statute is given a section number and may be divided into subsections.

To get a start on federal statutory citation form, look at the citations analyzed in B12.1.1 and Rule 12 of *The Bluebook*. The basic "formula" for a federal statute citation follows:

Title U.S.C. § Section (Date).

Rule 12.3.1(a) tells you to include the official or popular name of a statute and original section number only if the statute is commonly known by its name or if the inclusion of that information would be helpful. In most cases, you may omit the name of the statute. However, the new text of B12.1.1 seems to imply that inclusion of the

---

[1] To add to the confusion, cases in West reporters sometimes present statute and rule citations in ALL CAPS. Do not copy wholesale citations you see in cases! West publications do not adhere to Bluebook form.

official name is always required. The authors suggest that writers use their judgment as to whether inclusion of the title is helpful.

Clean Water Act, 33 U.S.C. § 1314(a)(1) (2012).

Otherwise, the first required component of the citation is the title number, which is analogous to a case citation's volume number. In a federal statutory citation, the title number precedes the name of the code cited just as the volume number of a case reporter precedes the name of the reporter in a case citation. The section number(s) follows the abbreviated code just as the page number follows the abbreviated reporter name in a case citation:

123 U.S. 456

28 U.S.C. § 1291

You cite individual code sections by using a single section symbol (§) followed by the section number. Rule 6.2(c) tells you to insert a space between the section symbol and the section number. To indicate that you are citing to more than one numbered section, use a double section symbol (§§) followed by the section numbers. Rule 3.3(b) requires a single section symbol if citing to multiple subsections within one section; use a double section symbol if citing to multiple subsections within different sections. Rule 3.3(b) also tells you to indicate a span of consecutive sections or subsections by using a hyphen between the inclusive numbers. (*The Bluebook* does not allow for the use of "*et seq.*"). To cite to nonconsecutive sections or subsections, use a comma to separate the section numbers.

28 U.S.C. §§ 1331-1367, 1441-1452 (2012).

28 U.S.C. §§ 1331, 1441 (2012).

Note, however, that you do not use double section symbols when you are citing to multiple subsections within the same numbered section.

28 U.S.C. § 1367(a)-(b) (2012).

When citing multiple subsubsections of a statute, you will generally follow the same rules as those for citing sections. When dealing with subsubsections, you will not repeat digits or letters.

28 U.S.C. § 105(b)(1), (5)

19 U.S.C. § 1490(a)(1)(A)-(C)

NOT:

28 U.S.C. § 105(b)(1), (b)(5)

19 U.S.C. § 1490(a)(1)(A)-(a)(1)(C)

Look again at the full citations given above. The last element in each is a year in parentheses. The U.S.C. main volumes are published every six years. The code is kept up to date between complete publications by annual supplements. When you are researching and citing federal statutes, you must make sure that the statutory provisions you are using and citing are the ones currently in effect. If you are researching on a commercial database, note that references are to the *United States Code Annotated* or other unofficial code that is continuously updated.

If all of your cited material appears in the main volume, then you simply include the year the main volume was published. If all of your cited material appears in a supplement, then you indicate this by including the abbreviation "Supp." and the year the supplement was published. If your reader would need to consult both the main volume and the supplement, then you must include both pieces of information connected by an ampersand (&).

Title U.S.C. § Section (Year & Supp. Year).

You will need to also refer to T1.1 to make sure you are citing the appropriate code. T1.1 tells you to cite to the *United States Code* if the statute is found therein. (See the note in T1.1 beside the heading "Statutory compilations.") Otherwise, you may cite to the *United States Code Annotated, United States Code Service*, or *United States Code Unannotated*, in that order of preference.

If you do not have access to the print version of the *United States Code* or its unofficial counterparts, you may cite to the electronic version. This is increasingly common with statutes. Unlike court opinions, statutes do not have a fixed, permanent year. A given statute may be amended or supplemented through the years. Therefore, the year is a piece of information that has to be updated each time the statute is cited. If you access statutes through only electronic databases, you will also not have access to the current information about the year of the print statute. In that case, you would cite to the electronic version of the statute.

Citation to the electronic source differs only in the parenthetical. Rule 12.5(a) tells you that, rather than indicating the year of the main volume and/or supplement, you will give the date information provided by the electronic database. In an electronic database, statutes are updated on a rolling basis without set publication dates of volumes and pocket parts. Electronic databases tell you how current the statute is that you are reading on your computer screen with language such as "current through the 2015 legislative session." You add this information, plus any commercial publisher's name, and the name of the database in the date parenthetical.

42 U.S.C. A. § 1983 (Westlaw through P.L. 113-296 (excluding P.L. 113-235, 113-287, and 113-291)).

Notice that the statutory compilation abbreviation is for the United States Code Annotated. This is because the Westlaw version would be the counterpart to the West print publication.

Because statutes are not assigned a unique database identifier, the short form for a statute found on an electronic database will look very similar to a short form for a statute found in a bound volume.

§ 1983.

Most, if not all, jursidictions' statutes can be found on government-sponsored web sites. When you believe that a parallel citation to the web site would improve access to the enacted law you are citing, rules B18 and 18 allow you to append the URL to the print source citation.

I.R.C. § 401 (2012), http://www.access.gpo.gov/congress/cong013.html.

Employee Retirement Income Security Act of 1974, 29 C.F.R. § 2510.3-1 (1999), http://www.dol.gov/dol/allcfr/Title_29/Part_2510/29CFR2510.3-1.htm.

Let's walk through a federal statutory citation to get you started. Let's put section 501 of title 17 of the *United States Code* into a citation sentence. Let's say that, when we look up subsection (a) of the statute, we find it in the 2014 Supplement, but all remaining provisions are in the main volume, published in 2012. We are not using the name of the act of which this statute is a part, so you know from Rule 12 that the first element of a federal statutory citation is the number of the title. In our statute, that number is 17. Next is the abbreviation of the code. Following the information on federal courts, T1.1 shows the proper abbreviations and formats for "Statutory compilations." You see that the abbreviation for the *United States Code* is "U.S.C." Rule B6 tells you to close up adjacent single capitals, so make sure there are no spaces in "U.S.C."

17 U.S.C.

Next comes a section symbol followed by a space. After the section symbol and space, you will insert the section number.

17 U.S.C. § 501

The final element is the year. You already know that the statute is currently in force and that you are citing the official code. Therefore, according to B12.1.1 and Rule 12.3.1(d), and as shown in T1.1, you do not have to show the name of a publisher. You know also that the main volumes of the current official code were published in 2012. The *United States Code* is kept up to date between complete publications by annual supplements numbered with roman numerals.[3] Because our statute is in both the main volume and supplement, both dates must be included.

Therefore, our finished citation sentence is the following:

17 U.S.C. § 501 (2012 & Supp. II 2014).

---

[3] The unofficial codes publish annual supplements for each separate volume. The supplements are inserted into pockets inside the back covers of the bound volumes and thus have come to be known as "pocket parts." When a pocket part becomes too bulky to fit conveniently into the pocket, the publisher puts out a softbound "cumulative supplement" which serves the same purpose but does not go inside the bound volume.

In addition to these rules for citing most statutes, you do need to know some rules for some specific statutes; these details are in Rule 12.9 and B12.1.3 through B12.1.5. For example, when citing to the current version of the Internal Revenue Code, you should cite to "I.R.C." rather than to title 26 of the *United States Code.*

I.R.C. § 703(a) (2012).

NOT:

26 U.S.C. § 703(a) (2012).

Similarly, B12.1.3 and Rule 12.9.3 tell us that cites to the current version of certain rules, such as the Federal Rules of Civil Procedure, which are published in an appendix to the *United States Code,* do not cite to the *United States Code,* but instead cite only to the rules themselves. A citation to the current version of the rule does not require a date parenthetical.

Fed. R. Civ. P. 26(b)(4).

Checklist for Federal Statutes

- If you are using the name of the statute, have you put that name first?

- Have you put the title number before the name of the code?

- Have you properly abbreviated the name of the code?

- Have you closed up (left no spaces between) all adjacent single capitals in the abbreviated name of the code?

- Have you inserted a single section symbol for a single statute and a double section symbol for more than one statute?

- Have you left a single space between the section symbol and the section number?

- Have you closed up the section number and its subsections?

- Have you put the year(s) of publication in parentheses at the end of your citation?

- If any portion of your cited material is included in a supplementary volume, have you indicated this in the date parenthetical?

- Have you left a space between the last character of the section number and the date parenthetical?

- Have you ended your citation sentence with a period?

Exercise 6
FEDERAL STATUTES

Put the following information in correct Bluebook citation form. All statutes are being cited in citation sentences. This exercise focuses on B11, B12.1.1, B12.1.3, B12.1.4, and B3, as well as Rules 11, 12.2, 12.3, 12.8, and 3.3(b). You will also need to refer to T1 for information on federal statutes. For each question, you must use the correct typeface given in B2 and the correct spacing given in B6 and 6.2(c).

1. Article three, section two, clause two of the Constitution of the United States.

_____

_____

2. Section 104 of title 11 of the current *United States Code*, published in the 2016 Supplement IV.

_____

_____

3. Subsections (a)(5) through (a)(6) of section 113 of title 18 of the current *United States Code*, published in the 2012 main volume.

_____

_____

4. Subsections (j)(1) and (j)(5) of section 941 of title 47 of the current *United States Code*. These sections appear in their entirety in the 2012 main volume.

_____

_____

5. Subsection (b)(3) of section 1070a of title 20 of the current *United States Code*, published in Supplement I in 2013.

_____

_____

6. Section 5128 of title 2 of the current *United States Code*. This section appears in its entirety in Supplement II, published in 2013.

_____

_____

7. Subsection (b)(1) of section 862 of title 21 of the current *United States Code*, published in the 2012 main volume.

_____

_____

8. Rule 56(b) of the current Federal Rules of Civil Procedure, published in 2012 in the Appendix to title 28 of the *United States Code*

---

9. Subsection (b)(1)(A) of section 1361 of the current Internal Revenue Code, published in the 2012 main volume for title 26 of the current *United States Code*. Use the special citation form for tax law provisions.

---

10. Rule 4(a) of the Federal Rules of Appellate Procedure, published in 2012 in the Appendix to title 28 of the *United States Code*.

Chapter 7

STATE STATUTES

> Before reading the chapter, read Bluepages rules B11, B12.1.2, B12.1.3, B12.1.4, and main body rules 11, 12.1.-12.3, and 12.5. Remember to space the statute abbreviation using B6.

Citation to state statutes is just as easy as federal statutes, even though each state has its own statutory compilation. Remember from Chapter 6, Federal Statutes, that B12 and B2 tells us that all text in the statute citation should be in ordinary roman type for legal memoranda and court documents, not large and small capitals as indicated by Rule 12. The key to state statute citation is each state's section of T1.3. In that section, the "formula" for that state is given. Generally, each citation will include the following:

- an abbreviated name of the state code (just as with the U.S.C., the name of the code will not use LARGE AND SMALL CAPITAL LETTERS)

- possibly the name of a subject matter if the code is arranged by subject matter;

- numerical information pointing the reader to a specific statutory provision;

- possibly the publisher of the code; and

- the year of publication.

In each state's entry in T1.3, you will find a template for what information to include and in what form. This table also includes the proper abbreviation for each state code. Therefore, for each state statute that you cite, you should always refer to that state's page in T1.3 for a fool-proof "formula." You may also need to consult Rule B6 to ensure that you are spacing the abbreviation correctly.

Most statutes are not organized by pages as cases are. Instead, most statutes are arranged by sections, but may also be arranged by chapters, titles, paragraphs, subdivisions, or a combination thereof. Therefore, in addition to consulting T1.3, you will also need to pay attention to Rule 3.3 with regard to sections and paragraphs. Broadly, remember that you indicate that you are citing to multiple sections by using two section symbols without a space in between. Note, however, that you need a space between the section symbol and the actual section number.

Ariz. Rev. Stat. Ann. §§ 17-454, 17-456 (2006).

Del. Code Ann. tit. 3, § 10105(a) (2001).

Alaska Stat. § 37.14.400 (2006).

The only other detail you need to know to master the basics of state statute citation is how to determine the date of the code. Note that the year of the code is NOT the date the particular statute was enacted. To avoid this confusion, remember the purpose of the date in the citation: to help your reader know how to find a particular statute. To do this, your reader must know what version of a code to consult, *i.e.*, the version of the code published in a particular year. In addition, your reader must know whether the information is contained in the main body of the code, a supplement or pocket part, or both. Therefore, you need to include this information. Generally, the year of the code will appear on the spine of the volume, the title page, or elsewhere as a copyright date. *The Bluebook* tells you to use the date appearing in one of these places, in the preceding order of preference. If the entirety of the section that you are citing appears in the main volume, use only the date for the main volume.

Del. Code Ann. tit. 7, § 931 (2001).

Often, part or all of the section will have been amended and reprinted in a supplementary volume that is either bound separately from the main volume or attached in a pocket located in the inside back cover of the main volume. In that case, include the years for both the main volume and the supplement.

Del. Code Ann. tit. 7, § 927 (2001 & Supp. 2015).

Many times, a newly enacted statute will appear only in the supplement or pocket part. In these cases, you should only include the year of the supplement, preceded by "Supp." pursuant to Rule 3.1(c).

Del. Code Ann. tit. 7, § 517(c) (Supp. 2015).

Some states, such as California and Michigan, have more than one statutory compilation. Generally, *The Bluebook* prefers citations to the official state code, if possible. T1.3 informs you which compilation to cite to in order of preference. However, most law libraries only subscribe to one set of state statutes for each state. Some compilations require you to include the publisher in the date parenthetical. If so, the publisher would be included in the formula given in T1.1

Alaska Stat. § 37.14.400 (1998).

Finally, states such as Texas and New York with subject matter codes use a "formula" that indicates where the subject of the code should be "plugged in" to the citation. The names of the subjects are abbreviated according to T6.

Tex. [subject] Code Ann. § x (West year).

The brackets indicate the place holder for the name of the subject; once the subject is included, the brackets are omitted.

Tex. Gov't Code Ann. § x (West year).

NOT:

Tex [Gov't] Code Ann. § x (West year).

Like federal statutes, state statutes may also be cited electronically. If you do not have access to the print version of the code you are citing, you may cite to the electronic version. This is increasingly common with statutes. Unlike court opinions, statutes do not have a fixed, permanent year. A given statute may be amended or supplemented through the years. Therefore, the year is a piece of information that has to be updated each time the statute is cited. If you access statutes through only electronic databases, you will also not have access to the current information about the year of the print statute. In that case, you would cite to the electronic version of the statute.

Citation to the electronic source differs only in the parenthetical. Rather than indicating the year of the main volume and/or supplement, you will give the date information provided by the electronic database. In an electronic database, statutes are updated on a rolling basis without set publication dates of volumes and pocket parts. Electronic databases tell you how current the statute is that you are reading on your computer screen with language such as "current through the 2015 Special Session." You add this information, plus any commercial publisher's name if required by T1, and the name of the database to the date parenthetical.

Wash. Rev. Code Ann. § 9.41.280(1)(a) (West, Westlaw through 2015 Spec. Sess.).

Notice that, even though the information provided reads "**the** 2015 Special Session," all examples in *The Bluebook* omit "the." Also notice that *The Bluebook* examples abbreviate legislative document terms. Therefore, follow the example above, and 1) do not include "the" in the completed citation, and 2) abbreviate any words found in T9.

Because statutes are not assigned a unique database identifier, the short form for a statute found in an electronic database will look very similar to a short form for a statute found in a bound volume.

§ 9.41.280(1)(a).

Checklist for State Statutes

- Have you consulted T1.3 for the correct abbreviation of the state code?

- Have you followed the format for the state statute given in T1.3?

- Have you taken the year of the code from the spine, title page, or copyright information in the appropriate volume?

- Does all of the information cited appear in the main volume?

  - If so, then include only the year of the main volume in the parenthetical.

  - If a portion of the statute cited is in a supplement, then include the date of the main volume and the supplement.

- Does all of the information cited appear in a supplement? If so, then include the date of only the supplement.

- For states with subject matter codes, have you omitted the brackets used in the T1.3 formula and abbreviated according to T6?

Exercise 7
STATE STATUTES

Put the following information in correct *Bluebook* citation form. All statutes are being cited in citation sentences. Although this exercise builds on the rules used in previous exercises, this exercise focuses on state rather than federal statutes. You will need to refer to T1 for information on the statutes in the appropriate jurisdiction. For each question, you must use the correct typeface given in B2 and the correct spacing given in B6 and Rule 6.2.

1. Section 10-9C-302 of *Michie's Alabama Code, 1975*, published by LexisNexis. This new provision appears entirely in the 2018 cumulative supplement.

2. Subsection 411.402(4) of *Michie's Kentucky Revised Statutes Annotated*, published by LexisNexis. The entire text of this subsection appears in the 2018 supplement.

3. Subsection 97-25-49(1)(b) of the *Mississippi Code 1972 Annotated*, published by LexisNexis. The entire text of this subsection appears in the 2012 main volume.

4. Subsections 13:17-52(a)–(c) of the *New Jersey Statutes Annotated*, published by West. The copyright date on the main volume is 2015. No amendments to this section appear in any supplement or pocket part and no other date appears on the main volume.

5. Sections 11-9-650 through 11-9-660 of the *Code of Laws of South Carolina 1976 Annotated*. Part of these sections appear in the 1986 main volume, and part appear in the 2018 cumulative supplement.

6. Sections 5-809(a) and (c) of the State Finance and Procurement subject code of *Michie's Annotated Code of Maryland*, published by LexisNexis. Both of these subsections appear in their entirety in the main volume, published in 2013.

7. Section 1215, subsection (a) of the *California Insurance Code*, part of *West's Annotated California Codes*. The entire text of subsection (a) appears in the main volume, published in 2013.

---

8. Section 25-1-801, subsections (2) and (4), of *West's Colorado Revised Statutes Annotated*. The date on the title of the main volume is 2008. This entire section appears in the 2013 supplement.

---

9. Section 2-317, subsections (a) through (c) of Chapter 106 of the *Annotated Laws of Massachusetts*, published by LexisNexis. You do not have the Massachusetts code available in print in your office; however, you do have a subscription to Lexis Advance. Therefore, you wish to cite the electronic version of the statute. The online version reports that it is current "through Act 176 of the 2017 Legislative Session."

---

10. Title 10, sections 1408(A) and 1415(B) of the *Oklahoma Statutes*, published by West. You do not have the Oklahoma code available in print in your office; however, you do have a subscription to Westlaw. Therefore, you wish to cite the electronic version of the statute. The online version reports that it is current "through the First Regular Session and the First Special Session of the 56th Legislature."

---

11. Article 2337 of *West's Louisiana Civil Code Annotated*. You do not have the Louisiana code available in print in your office; however, you do have a subscription to Westlaw. Therefore, you wish to cite the electronic version of the statute. The online version reports that it is current "through the 2017 Second Extraordinary Session."

---

12. Section 3153 of title 23 of *West's Main Statutes*. You do not have the Maine code available in print in your office; however, you do have a subscription to Westlaw. Therefore, you wish to cite the electronic version of the statute. The online version reports that it is current "through Chapter 312 and RR 2017 Chapter 1 of the 2017 First Regular of the 128th Legislature."

---

13. Section 1105, subsections (a), (c), and (e), of title 3 of the *Delaware Code Annotated*, published by LexisNexis. You do not have the Delaware code available in print in your office; however, you do have a subscription to Lexis Advance. Therefore, you wish to cite the electronic version of the statute. The online version reports that it is current "through 81 Del. Laws, chapter 199."

_____

_____

14. Section 28-b(3), subsection (a)(1), of the Banking Law subject code of *McKinney's Consolidated Laws of New York Annotated*, published by West. You do not have the New York code available in print in your office; however, you do have a subscription to Lexis Advance. Therefore, you wish to cite the electronic version of the statute. The online version reports that it is current "through 2018 Chapter 1."

_____

_____

15. Sections 21-4217 and 21-4219 of the *Kansas Statutes Annotated*, published by the state government of Kansas. You do not have the Kansas code available in print in your office; however, you do have a subscription to Lexis Advance. Therefore, you wish to cite the electronic version of the statute. The online version reports that it is current "through the 2017 Regular Session."

_____

_____

Chapter 8

SHORT FORMS (STATUTES)

Before reading the chapter, read Bluepages rules B4, B11, B12.2, and main body rules 4, 11 and 12.10. Remember to space the statute abbreviation using B6.

As with cases, you will often refer to a statute several times within a legal memorandum or a court document. Similarly, *The Bluebook* states that you need to give the full legal citation for a statute only the *first* time that you cite to that statute. As long as subsequent references to the same statute appear in the same general discussion, you may use a short form citation to that statute. B12.2 and Rules 4.1(b) and 12.10 provide information on short form citations for state and federal statutes. (Note that the last rule in each chapter generally deals with short forms for sources discussed within that chapter.) The chart included in Rule 12.10 is a handy reference that is well worth flagging in some way. B11 and Rule 11 tell us that the only acceptable short form for a constitution is "*id.*" Otherwise, use the full form.

As with cases, *The Bluebook* provides two types of short forms to be used for statutes in legal memoranda and court documents: "*id.*" and an abbreviated version of the full legal citation. The rules for when you may use each type parallel the rules that we discussed in connection with cases. You may use the short form "*id.*" only when you are citing to a statute previously cited in the immediately preceding citation (and only if that previous citation is not a string cite). Again, no intervening cites to a different authority of any type should appear between the previous cite to this statute and the current citation.

You learned in Exercise 5 (Short Forms (Cases)) that you use "*id.*" to refer to a previous case even when you want to cite to a different page. Similarly, the previous citation to a statute need not be to the exact section or subsection of your statute; however, you will need to include any information in your citation that differs from the immediately preceding citation. Unlike case short forms, however, statutory short forms never use the word "at," as detailed in Rule 3.3. The proper formulation is simply the word "*id.*" followed immediately by the new section or subsection information. Because Rule 4.1 tells you that you should indicate in an "*id.*" cite only the way in which that citation differs from the previous one, you will omit the code abbreviation and the date and publisher parenthetical, provided that the material is the same for the "*id.*" cite as for the original citation. However, you should reproduce the entire section number for clarity. Notice in the example below that the second citation includes both the section and subsection information rather than just the different subsection. Notice that the third citation includes also the date parenthetical because section 1–201(b)(4) is in the 2015 Supplement, but the original section cited was in the 2010 main volume.

> In our jurisdiction, "fruit" is defined as an edible part of a plant that contains seeds. **St. Stat. Ann.** § 1–201(a) (2010). A "vegetable" is defined as an edible part of a plant that does not contain seeds. *Id.* § 1-201(b)(1). However, the term "vegetable" does not include legumes or tubers. *Id.* Recently, the legislature determined that a cucumber, although it contains seeds, would be deemed to be a vegetable. *Id.* § 1-201(b)(4) **(Supp. 2015).**

In those circumstances when you wish to use a short form but cannot use "*id.,*" you will use an abbreviated form of the full citation. Rule 12.10 provides a chart of acceptable short forms, and B12.2 incorporates the chart by reference. For federal statutes, you may retain the volume and abbreviation for the *United States Code* in addition to the section number or retain only the section number.

> 36 U.S.C. § 301 (2012).

> becomes:

> 36 U.S.C. § 301.

> OR

> § 301.

Depending on the compilation strategy of a particular state code, you may not have many options in composing your short form; at other times, you may have an option as to how much information to retain, as in the *Delaware Code Annotated* example in the chart included in Rule 12.10. Generally, you omit all references to the name of the code and the date of publication information and retain all numerical information relating to the statute. For instance, if the state code is organized only by sections, such as the *Maryland Code*, then you simply omit the code name information and retain the section number.

> Md. Code Ann., Fin. Inst. § 13–708.1 (West 2003).

> becomes:

> § 13–708.1.

However, some state codes, such as *General Laws of the Commonwealth of Massachusetts*, are divided into titles or chapters and then further into sections. For those state statutes, you may retain all of the numerical information or merely the section number.

> Mass. Gen. Laws ch. 4, § 7 (Supp. 2015).

> becomes:

> Ch. 4, § 7.

> OR

§ 7.

If the state code is organized and named by subject matter, then you would retain the subject-matter abbreviation in the short form.

Cal. Fin. Code § 40021(b) (West Supp. 2014).

becomes:

Fin. § 40021(b).

You will eventually develop your own preference, but your ultimate objective should be absolute clarity for your reader.

Checklist for Statutory Short Forms

- Did you cite to the current statute in the immediately preceding citation? If not, then you cannot use *"id."*

- Does the immediately preceding citation contain more than one authority, *i.e.*, is it a string cite? If so, then you cannot use *"id."*

- If you cannot use *"id.,"* have you formulated an acceptable abbreviated short form?

- Have you remembered not to include the word "at" in your short form?

Exercise 8
SHORT FORMS (STATUTES)

Put the following information in correct *Bluebook* citation form. All statutes are being cited in citation sentences. Although this exercise builds on the rules used in previous exercises, this exercise focuses on B11 and B12, specifically B12.2, and Rules 4.1, 11, and 12.10. You will need to refer to T1 for information on the statutes in the appropriate jurisdiction. For each question, you must use the correct typeface given in B2 and the correct spacing given in B6 and Rule 6.2.

1. In the immediately preceding sentence of a legal memorandum, you cited to a provision in the *North Dakota Century Code*, N.D. Cent. Code § 44-08-19(1) (2017). Without an intervening cite, you wish to cite to subsection (2) of this same statute.

   _____

2. In the same general discussion of your memorandum, after citing to several cases, you wish to cite again to N.D. Cent. Code § 44-08-19(1) (2017).

   _____

3. In the very next sentence of your memorandum, without an intervening cite, you wish to cite to the same subsection (1) described in Problem 2.

   _____

4. Earlier in the same general discussion, you cited to 10 U.S.C. § 3741(3) (2012). Now, two pages later, you wish to cite to subsection (1). Several cites to cases appear on the two intervening pages. You have been referring to this section in text as "Section 3741."

   _____

5. In another memorandum, you cited to a provision of *Michie's Annotated Code of Maryland*, Md. Code Ann., State Fin. & Proc. § 12-202(b) (LexisNexis 2015). In the next line, you again cite to the same provision, using a short form. In the next paragraph, without any intervening cites, you wish to cite to subsection (d) of the same provision.

   _____

6. In the same paragraph of the memorandum mentioned in Problem 5, following a cite to a case construing subsection (d), you wish to cite to Md. Code Ann., State Fin. & Proc. § 12-202(e) (LexisNexis 2015).

_____

_____

7. In an appellate brief, you wish to cite to section 14-40 of the *General Statutes of Connecticut*. The immediately preceding cite reads "Conn. Gen. Stat. § 14-53 (2012); *New Haven College, Inc. v. Zoning Bd. of Appeals*, 227 A.2d 427 (Conn. 1967).

_____

_____

8. In a legal memorandum, you have previously cited to Mich. Comp. Laws Ann. § 567.250(2) (West Supp. 2018). A few paragraphs later, with several intervening cites to cases, you wish to cite to subsection (1).

_____

_____

9. In the next sentence of the memorandum described in Problem 8, without any intervening cites, you wish to cite to Mich. Comp. Laws Ann. § 567.250(2) (West Supp. 2018).

_____

_____

10. In a legal memorandum, you have previously cited to a portion of the United States Constitution, U.S. Const. art. II, § 1. After several intervening cites to other authorities, you wish to cite to the same provision.

_____

_____

Chapter 9

COMPREHENSIVE CORE EXERCISE

After completing the first eight exercises, you are well on your way to mastering legal citation! Let's stop, catch our breath, and review what you have learned.

By now, you should know how to cite any case decided by a court in the United States, whether state or federal. Also, if you are citing a case to a state court and that state requires parallel citation to a state reporter and a regional reporter, you know how to construct that parallel citation. You also know how to use "*id.*" and how to formulate short forms for case citations.

Similarly, you know how to cite to any statute, state or federal. You are also comfortable using "*id.*" and short forms to refer to statutes that you have already referenced in a full citation.

With these skills, you can cite to most authoritative sources and produce a professional legal memorandum or court document. In the next exercises, we are going to introduce you to the concept of citation signals, which "signal" to your reader the importance of citations if the connection between the source and your proposition is not clear in the text alone. You will also learn how to add explanatory parentheticals to your citations to reinforce and clarify the importance of those citations. We will also explore other types of sources, such as books, treatises, law review articles, and legislative resources.

Before we continue marching on, you may want to try Exercise 9: Comprehensive Core Exercise, which will reinforce the skills learned in Exercises 1–8. To help you get back into the swing of things, the following is a list of common mistakes first-year law students make in basic citation:

- Forgetting to put a court designation in the court and date parenthetical when the reporter information is not sufficient.

- Guessing on the abbreviations in case names instead of checking T6.

- Omitting the volume and reporter information in a case short form: *e.g.*, "*Casper*, 99 U.S. at 310," **not** "*Casper*, at 310."

- Omitting the comma between the case name and the volume information in a case short form.

- Omitting the space between "F." and "Supp." and "Supp." and "2d" for cases reported in *Federal Supplement* ("F. Supp." and "F. Supp. 2d").

- Omitting a date parenthetical in a full citation of a statute.

Finally, remember your successful completion of these exercises does not mean that you should never consult *The Bluebook* again. Most student citation mistakes arise when students think they remember what *The Bluebook* says, but do not actually look up the rule. The best legal writers are not those who memorize *The Bluebook*, but those who know when to open it.

Exercise 9
COMPREHENSIVE CORE EXERCISE

Put the following information in correct *Bluebook* citation form. Assume that the authority is being cited in citation sentences in a brief to the United States Supreme Court unless otherwise noted. For each question, you must use the correct typeface given in B2 and the correct spacing given in B6 and Rule 6.2. This exercise reviews the skills you learned in Exercises 1 through 8.

1. The Estate of Joseph L. Haskins, deceased, Lloyd L. Edwards and Jayne C. Haskins, Executors, versus the United States of America. This case was decided in the United States Court of Appeals for the Ninth Circuit on February 28, 1966. It appears in volume 357, page 492, of *Federal Reporter*. You wish to direct your reader to information on page 493.

_____

_____

2. On page 4 of a legal memorandum, you cited to the case in Problem 1. In the same general discussion on page 6, you would like to refer to this case again, focusing your reader's attention on information beginning on page 493 of the opinion and continuing through page 496. You have cited to other cases in the interim. You have been referring to the case in text as *Estate of Haskins*. [For your reference, the text of Problem 1 is: The Estate of Joseph L. Haskins, deceased, Lloyd L. Edwards and Jayne C. Haskins, Executors, versus the United States of America. This case was decided in the United States Court of Appeals for the Ninth Circuit on February 28, 1966. It appears in volume 357, page 492, of *Federal Reporter*. You wish to direct your reader to information on page 493.]

_____

_____

3. Section 13:1K-20 of the *New Jersey Statutes Annotated*, published by West. The date on the copyright page is 2003, no other date appears on the volume and no amendments appear in any pocket part or supplement.

_____

_____

4. You wish to cite again to section 13:1K-20 of the *New Jersey Statutes Annotated* in the next paragraph of an appellate brief. You have cited to two cases since your last reference to section 13:1K-20.

_____

_____

5. Cage Realty, Inc., Appellant, versus Hugh A. and Marguerite J. Hanna, Respondents. This case was decided in the Missouri Court of Appeals on August 16, 1994. It appears in volume 881, page 254, of *South Western Reporter*, Second Series.

_____

_____

6. Section 773(a)(2)(A) of title 29 of the *United States Code*, published in its entirety in the 2012 main volume.

_____

_____

7. One paragraph later, after citing to a provision of the United States Constitution, you wish to cite again to Section 773(a)(2)(A) of title 29 of the *United States Code*, the same section described in Problem 6. You have been referring to this section as "Section 773(a)(2)(A)."

_____

_____

8. Subsections 571.0771(c)(1) through (c)(3) of the *Texas Government Code*, a subject code that is part of *Vernon's Texas Codes Annotated*, published by West. This section appears in its entirety in the 2011 main volume.

_____

_____

9. Beverly California Corporation, a California corporation, doing business as Applegate East Nursing Home, Appellant, versus Donna E. Shalala, Secretary of Health and Human Services; Chester Stroyny, Administrator, Region V, Health Care Financing Administration of the U.S. Department of Health and Human Services, Appellees. This case was decided by the United States Court of Appeals for the Eighth Circuit on March 13, 1996. It appears in volume 78, page 403, of *Federal Reporter*, Third Series.

_____

_____

10. Nationsbanc Mortgage Corporation versus Paul K. Eisenhauer and Mary E. Eisenhauer. This case was decided by the Appeals Court of Massachusetts on July 27, 2000. It appears in volume 49, page 727, of *Massachusetts Appeals Court Reports* and in volume 733, page 557, of *North Eastern Reporter*, Second Series. You are citing this case in a brief to the Massachusetts Supreme Judicial Court. Assume that the usual practice in Massachusetts is to cite both state and regional reporters, in that order.

_____

_____

11. You wish to refer to the case from Problem 10 in the next sentence of your brief, without any intervening citations. However, this time you would like to direct your reader's attention to information found on page 728 of *Massachusetts Appeals Court Reports* and on page 559 of *North Eastern Reporter*, Second Series. [For your reference, the text of Problem 10 is: Nationsbanc Mortgage Corporation versus Paul K. Eisenhauer and Mary E. Eisenhauer. This case was decided by the Appeals Court of Massachusetts on July 27, 2000. It appears in volume 49, page 727, of *Massachusetts Appeals Court Reports* and in volume 733, page 557, of *North Eastern Reporter*, Second Series. You are citing this case in a brief to the Massachusetts Supreme Judicial Court. Assume that the usual practice in Massachusetts is to cite both state and regional reporters, in that order.]

12. The current text of Federal Rule of Civil Procedure 12(b)(6), published in 2012 in the appendix to title 18 of the *United States Code*.

13. Section 70/4 of chapter 410 of *West's Smith-Hurd Illinois Compiled Statutes Annotated*. The entire provision appears in the 2011 main volume.

14. The People of California versus Wendell W. Shaw. This case was decided by the District Court of Appeal of California on September 18, 1941. This case appears in volume 46, page 768, of *California Appellate Reports*, Second Series, and in volume 177, page 34, of *Pacific Reporter*, Second Series. You are citing this case in an appellate brief in a state court in Oregon. Assume Oregon has no local rule concerning the citation of out-of-state cases.

15. You wish to cite to the case from Problem 14 two pages later in your brief, after several intervening cites. You want to direct your reader's attention to information that appears on page 769 of the state reporter and page 35 of the regional reporter. You have been referring to this case in text as *"Shaw."* [For your reference, the text of Problem 14 is: The People of California versus Wendell W. Shaw. This case was decided by the District Court of Appeal of California on September 18, 1941. This case appears in volume 46, page 768, of *California Appellate Reports*, Second Series, and in volume 177, page 34, of *Pacific Reporter*, Second Series. You are citing this case in an appellate brief in a state court in Oregon. Assume Oregon has no local rule concerning the citation of out-of-state cases.]

16. The Wisconsin State Employees Association Council 24 versus the Wisconsin Natural Resources Board. This case was decided by the United States District Court for the District of Columbia in 1969. It appears in volume 298, page 339, of *Federal Supplement*.

_____

_____

17. Section 968.26 of *West's Wisconsin Statutes Annotated*. You accessed it online on Westlaw, which tells you that the provision online is current "through 2017 Act 135, published December 12, 2017."

_____

_____

18. In the next sentence, without any intervening cites, you wish to cite to subsection (3) of section 968.26. (In Problem 17, you cited the whole of section 968.26.) This subsection has the same currency information as the section itself.

_____

_____

19. Odessa Fay Howard, Respondent, versus Handler Bros. & Winell, Inc., Appellant. This case was decided by the Court of Appeals of New York on April 23, 1952. It appears in volume 106, page 67, of *North Eastern Reporter*, Second Series, and in volume 303, page 990, of *New York Reports*. You are citing this case in a brief to the Supreme Court, Appellate Division, of New York. Assume that the usual practice in New York is to cite both state and regional reporters, in that order.

_____

_____

20. City of Miami versus J.C. Nelson, a minor, by his mother and next friend, Clara Nelson, and Clara Nelson, individually. This case was decided by the District Court of Appeal of Florida on March 15, 1966. It appears in volume 186, page 535, of *Southern Reporter*, Second Series. You wish to focus your reader's attention to information on page 537.

_____

_____

Chapter 10

PRIOR & SUBSEQUENT CASE HISTORY

> Before reading the chapter, read Bluepages rule B10.1.6, and main body rules 10.7, including all subsections.

Now that you have mastered a basic case citation, you are ready to add a more advanced skill: prior and subsequent history. You probably have learned by now that one case may go through several levels of appeal in its life. At each level, the court reviewing the case may publish an opinion. Opinions issued by courts that review the case after the opinion you wish to cite are called *subsequent history*. Opinions issued by courts before the opinion you wish to cite are called *prior history*. The rules for citing prior and subsequent history tend to be fairly detailed and complex, but remember: you need not memorize any citation rules. You only need to understand how they work and where to find them so you can refresh your understanding.

To illustrate this, let's use the fictional case of *Bait v. Switch*. *Bait v. Switch* started out as a negligence lawsuit in federal trial court in the Northern District of Texas. Bait was awarded damages by the trial court, and the trial court issued an opinion. This opinion was reported in *Federal Supplement*. Switch then appealed to the Fifth Circuit Court of Appeals. The Fifth Circuit affirmed the trial court's judgment and also issued an opinion, which was published in *Federal Reporter*, Third Series. Finally, Switch filed a writ of certiorari to the United States Supreme Court. The United States Supreme Court denied certiorari, issuing an opinion explaining the reason for the denial. This opinion was reported in several reporters, including *United States Reports*. So we have three different courts that have dealt with this case and issued opinions. The Fifth Circuit Court of Appeals and United States Supreme Court opinions are *subsequent history* to the federal trial court opinion.

$$\boxed{\text{N.D. Tex.}} \qquad \text{5th Cir.} \qquad \text{U.S.}$$

subsequent history

The federal trial court and Fifth Circuit opinions are *prior history* to the United States Supreme Court opinion.

The Fifth Circuit opinion has both prior and subsequent history—the federal district court opinion is prior history, and the United States Supreme Court opinion is

N.D. Tex.   5th Cir. | U.S. |

prior history

subsequent history.

N.D. Tex. | 5th Cir. | U.S.

prior history   **subsequent history**

You will find citations to prior and subsequent history by using a citator service such as *Shepard's*. You should receive instruction on how to use a citator in your legal research class.

The rule governing when to include prior and subsequent history is Rule 10.7. As we will see shortly, you also will need to consult Rule 10.5(d) sometimes when including prior or subsequent history. *The Bluebook* tells us first **when** to include prior and subsequent history and then **how** to include it.

"When" is covered in Rule 10.7. The general rule for subsequent history is that it should be included when you cite a decision in full. (This means, then, that short cites should not include prior or subsequent history.) However, this is a rule with many exceptions. And the exceptions have exceptions.

Include subsequent history unless . . .

- **the history is a denial of certiorari or similar discretionary appeal**

  but include denials of cert. if the decision is less than two years old or "the denial is particularly relevant,"

- **the history is on remand or the denial of a rehearing**

  but include this type of history if it is particularly relevant to the point cited, or

- **the history is a disposition that has been withdrawn by the deciding authority.**

The general rule for prior history is that it *should not* be included. This rule also has exceptions, but they are a little easier to remember.

Do not include prior history unless . . .

- **the history is "significant to the point for which the case is cited" or**

- **the decision cited does not "intelligibly describe the issues in the case."**

When would a decision not "intelligibly describe" the issue? Let's go back to *Bait v. Switch*. Assume we want to cite the Fifth Circuit's opinion in *Bait v. Switch* because it is favorable to the point we are arguing. However, the Fifth Circuit opinion does not include as full a description of the facts in the case as the district court opinion does. If we wanted to analogize our facts closely to those of *Bait v. Switch* to argue that our client's case should be decided the same way the Fifth Circuit decided *Bait*, we might give the prior history of *Bait v. Switch* (the federal district court opinion) so we could use the lower court's description of the facts.

So now that we know **when** to give prior and subsequent history, we're ready to learn **how** to do it. Rule 10.7.1(a) tells us that the prior or subsequent history will follow the full citation of the primary case. This usually means that the history cite will follow the primary cite's court and date parenthetical. However, if the primary case cite includes an additional parenthetical (for explanation, weight of authority, etc.—all things we will cover in Chapter 12), then the history cite follows that parenthetical.

Our history cite will be introduced by an explanatory phrase. A partial list of these explanatory phrases appears in T8. Notice in T8 that some of the phrases are followed by commas and others are not. If the phrase is not followed by a comma in T8, then do not place a comma after it in your citation. Notice also that some of the phrases are (or begin with) an *-ing* verb while others begin with an *-ed* verb. The *-ing* verbs introduce prior history and are not followed by a comma; the *-ed* verbs introduce subsequent history and are followed by a comma.

These explanatory phrases give the reader important information about the relationship between the cases cited. For example, what if we want to cite *Bait v. Switch* (the district court opinion) for Proposition A, but it has been reversed in *Switch v. Bait* (the Fifth Circuit opinion) for the lower court's error on Proposition B? Although *Bait v. Switch* is no longer good law for Proposition B, it is still good law for Proposition A. To let the reader know that we are aware of the reversal but that it has no impact on our argument, we would introduce the subsequent history cite with the explanatory phrase *"rev'd on other grounds."*

When including history, pay close attention to the date of decision for all of the cases in the citation. If two cases listed consecutively in the cite are decided in the same year, then Rule 10.5(d) tells us to note the year only in the final court and date parenthetical containing that year. What if we have three citations: the primary cite in Year A, the first subsequent history cite also in Year A, and a final subsequent history cite in Year B? In that case, include no date of decision for the primary cite, Year A as the date of decision in the first history cite, and Year B as the date of decision in the final history cite.

North v. South, 111 Rptr. 222 **(Ct.)**, *rev'd*, 333 Rptr. 444 **(Ct. Year A)**, *rev'd*, 555 Rptr. 666 **(Ct. Year B)**.

Sometimes, a case requires several history citations. If we give both a prior and a subsequent history citation, Rule 10.7.1(a) tells us to list the prior history first. If we give several dispositions (either two or more prior history cites or two or more subsequent history cites), Rule 10.7.1(a) tells us to append those cites to each other, separating them with a comma. For an example, consult the *Herbert v. Lando* and *Kubrick v. United States* examples in Rule 10.7.1(a).

Most of the subsequent history will be in the cited case's direct line. For example, all of the opinions in the *Bait v. Switch* example involve the same parties and the same litigation. However, Rule 10.7.1(c) tells us to note as subsequent history cases that overrule a cited case, regardless of whether the cases are otherwise related.

What happens if the case name changes on appeal? Rule 10.7.2 covers this. If the names are simply reversed on appeal, then we do nothing. Cite the case name as it appears in the primary case we are citing and simply give a citation without a case name for the prior or subsequent history. The same is true if the history cite is a denial of certiorari or an administrative action in which the private party is the same.

But what if the first-named party changes on either or both sides? Not all parties that are involved in one phase of a case are necessarily involved in subsequent appeals. If we want to indicate a different name for a subsequent history cite, add the phrase "*sub nom.*" to the explanatory phrase and give the case name along with the citation for the history cite. If we want to indicate a different name for prior history, simply give the case names for both the primary and prior history cite, but do not introduce the second name with "*sub nom.*"

That's a lot of explanation, but the drafting is really not bad. Let's try an example. Because we are familiar with Bait and Switch, let's use their case and assume that we have the following citations to work with:

trial court:	*Bait v. Switch*, 111 F. Supp. 222 (N.D. Tex. 1994).
intermediate court of appeals:	*Switch v. Bait*, 333 F.3d 444 (5th Cir. 1994).
court of last resort:	*Switch v. Jones*, 555 U.S. 666 (1995).
unrelated case:	*Duck v. Cover*, 777 U.S. 888 (1997).

First, let's assume that we want to cite the intermediate court of appeals opinion in the Bait and Switch litigation. So, we start with that citation:

Switch v. Bait, 333 F.3d 444 (5th Cir. 1994).

We start with the general rule that we include subsequent history. So we consider whether to include the citation to *Switch v. Jones*. If *Switch v. Jones* was simply a denial of certiorari by the United States Supreme Court, we would not include it. Why? The decision in *Switch v. Bait* was issued more than two years prior to today's date, when we want to cite the 1994 decision. Therefore, the denial of certiorari would not be included. However, the Supreme Court did not deny certiorari. Instead, when we look up *Switch v. Jones*, we discover that the Supreme Court heard the case and issued an opinion affirming the Fifth Circuit's decision in *Switch v. Bait*. However, it affirmed the Fifth Circuit on different grounds from those for which we intend to cite the case. First, we will need to turn to T8 to find out what explanatory phrase to use. Sixth down from the top of the list, we see "*aff'd on other grounds*,"—that looks like exactly what we need. Remember that we use the *-ed* phrase because the phrase introduces subsequent history. Notice that we will replace the period at the end of the original citation sentence with a comma and save the period for the new end of our citation sentence.

Switch v. Bait, 333 F.3d 444 (5th Cir. 1994), *aff'd on other grounds*,

Notice also that T8 says to use a comma after this particular explanatory phrase. Remember, commas *following* italicized text are not italicized according to Rule 2.1(f).

Now it's time for the history citation. To name or not to name. Well, the party names are not simply reversed (*Switch v. Bait* and *Switch v. Jones*), and this is not a denial of certiorari or an administrative action. Rather, we have a subsequent history citation with a different name. So follow Rule 10.7.2. and add "*sub nom.*" to the explanatory phrase and then give the case name along with the other citation information. Notice that when you add "*sub nom.*" to the explanatory phrase, you omit any comma that would otherwise follow the phrase. This is one of those rules that is given by example rather than explicitly.

> *Switch v. Bait*, 333 F.3d 444 (5th Cir. 1994), *aff'd on other grounds sub nom.*
> *Switch v. Jones*, 555 U.S. 666 (1995).

Notice that we give the date of decision for both cites, because the decisions were in different years. Had they been in the same year (1995), then we would only give the year of decision in the second court and date parenthetical. It would look like this:

> *Switch v. Bait*, 333 F.3d 444 (5th Cir.), *aff'd on other grounds sub nom. Switch*
> *v. Jones*, 555 U.S. 666 (1995).

Let's try it the other way around: cite *Switch v. Jones* with *Switch v. Bait* as *prior* history. The same explanatory phrase will not work, so go back to T8. It looks like "*aff'g*" is what we want. Remember that we use the *-ing* form of the verb for prior history. Notice that "*aff'g*" is not followed by a comma.

> *Switch v. Jones*, 555 U.S. 666 (1995), *aff'g Switch v. Bait*, 333 F.3d 444 (5th Cir.
> 1994).

Now, let's cite the federal district court case *Bait v. Switch* with all its subsequent history. Remember that Rule 10.7.1(a) tells you to append consecutive prior or subsequent histories to one another, separating them with a comma. Let's assume that each court affirmed the court below it:

> *Bait v. Switch*, 111 F. Supp. 222 (N.D. Tex.), *aff'd*, 333 F.3d 444 (5th Cir. 1994),
> *aff'd sub nom. Switch v. Jones*, 555 U.S. 666 (1995).

Notice that we do not include a case name for the Fifth Circuit opinion because the name is just a reversal of the cite before it (the primary cite of *Bait v. Switch*). However, we do include the case name for *Switch v. Jones* because it names different parties than the lower court opinions. Notice also that we do not include the year of decision in the parenthetical for *Bait* v. Switch because the district court's decision was in the same year as the Fifth Circuit's decision.

Okay, one more twist on Messrs. Bait and Switch. Let's cite the Fifth Circuit opinion, giving both prior and subsequent history. Remember that Rule 10.7.1(a) tells us to include prior history first. Again, assume that the case was affirmed all the way up.

> *Switch v. Bait*, 333 F.3d 444 (5th Cir.), *aff'g* 111 F. Supp. 222 (N.D. Tex. 1994),
> *aff'd sub nom. Switch v. Jones*, 555 U.S. 666 (1995).

See? You're getting the hang of it! Let's assume that Bait, Switch, and Jones never went to the Supreme Court. They only got as far as the Fifth Circuit before they got tired of the whole thing. However, a few years later a similar case did go to the

Supreme Court, and the Supreme Court's opinion in that case (*Duck v. Cover*) explicitly overruled what the Fifth Circuit had to say in *Switch v. Bait*. That would be important history to note any time you cite *Switch v. Bait*. You would do that according to Rule 10.7.1(c):

> *Switch v. Bait*, 333 F.3d 444 (5th Cir. 1994), *overruled by Duck v. Cover*, 777 U.S. 888 (1997).

Notice that "*overruled by*" is not followed by a comma.

Okay, now you're ready to make history on your own! Because these rules are so detailed, you may find the following checklists especially helpful in completing the exercise.

Checklist for Subsequent Case History

- Is there any reason not to include subsequent history?
  - The answer is yes if the subsequent history citation is . . .
    - an irrelevant denial of certiorari on a decision older than two years,
    - an irrelevant history on remand or denial of rehearing, or
    - a decision withdrawn by the deciding authority.
  - Otherwise, continue . . .
- Have you replaced the period at the end of the primary citation with a comma (remember that the history cite follows the *entire* primary cite, even if the primary cite includes explanatory or other types of parentheticals)?
- Have you introduced your citation with an italicized explanatory phrase?
- Have you verified whether you need a comma after the explanatory phrase directly from or based on the phrases in T8?
- Do you need to include the case name in the history cite?
  - The answer is no if . . .
    - the party names are simply reversed,
    - the history cite is a denial of certiorari, or
    - the history cite is an administrative action with the same private parties.
  - Otherwise, include the case name.
- If you included a case name, have you added "*sub nom.*" to your explanatory phrase?
- If you added "*sub nom.*" to your explanatory phrase, have you omitted the comma following the explanatory phrase?
- If you included prior history in the citation as well, did you place the prior history first?
- Did you end your full citation sentence with a period?

Checklist for Prior Case History

- Do you need prior history at all?
  - Is the earlier case significant to the point the primary case is being cited for?
  - Does the earlier case better describe the issues than the primary case?
- Have you replaced the period at the end of the primary citation with a comma?
- Have you introduced your citation with an italicized explanatory phrase directly from or based on the phrases in T8?
- Have you verified whether you need a comma after the explanatory phrase?
- Do you need to include the case name in the history cite?

- The answer is no if . . .
  - the party names are simply reversed,
  - the history cite is a denial of certiorari, or
  - the history cite is an administrative action with the same private parties.
- Otherwise, include the case name.
- If you included subsequent history in the citation as well, did you place the prior history first?
- Did you end your full citation sentence with a period?

Exercise 10
PRIOR & SUBSEQUENT CASE HISTORY

Put the following information in correct *Bluebook* citation form. All cases are being cited in citation sentences in a brief to the United States Supreme Court. Although this exercise builds on the rules used in the previous exercises, this exercise focuses on B10.1.6 and Rules 10.7 and 10.5(d). Unless the problem states otherwise, you should assume that case names are the same at each level of appeal. Remember that you must decide *whether* to include a history cite before you decide how to cite it. The first case listed in each problem is the primary citation. Remember that each case name must be italicized according to B2.

1. You want to cite Robert Lee Stunzig, Jr., Petitioner, versus Jessica Flammer Koch, Respondent. This case is May 2017 case from the Eleventh Circuit Court of Appeals. It is reported in volume 687, page 841, of *Federal Appendix*. The United States Supreme Court denied certiorari on November 27, 2017. That denial is not yet reported in *United States Reports* but is reported in volume 138, page 473, of *Supreme Court Reporter*. The denial of certiorari is not relevant to the argument you are drafting.

_____

_____

_____

2. You want to cite Anti-Monopoly, Incorporated, Plaintiff, versus General Mills Fun Group, Incorporated, Defendant. This case is an August 26, 1982, federal case from the Ninth Circuit Court of Appeals published in volume 684, page 1316, of *Federal Reporter*, Second Series. The United States Supreme Court denied certiorari in 1983. The denial is published in volume 459, page 1227, of *United States Reports* and in volume 75, page 468, of *Lawyer's Edition*, Second Series. The denial of certiorari has no impact on the argument you are drafting.

_____

_____

_____

3. You want to cite Farmworker Justice Fund, Incorporated, et al., Petitioners, versus William E. Brock, Secretary of Labor, et al., Respondents. This is a 1987 federal case from the United States Court of Appeals, District of Columbia Circuit, published in volume 811, page 613, of *Federal Reporter*, Second Series. The D.C. Circuit vacated this decision as being moot in a 1987 opinion published in volume 817, page 890, of *Federal Reporter*, Second Series.

_____

_____

_____

4. You want to cite Interstellar Starship Services, Limited, versus Epix, Incorporated, an Illinois Corporation. This is a 1997 federal case from the United States District Court, District of Oregon, published in volume 983, page 1331, *Federal Supplement*. In January 1999 the Ninth Circuit Court of Appeals reversed the district court's decision in an opinion published in volume 184, page 1107, *Federal Reporter*, Second Series. Interstellar Starship applied for a writ of certiorari that was denied by the United States Supreme Court in 2000. That denial appears in volume 528, page 1155, of *United States Reports*. The denial of certiorari has no impact on the argument you are drafting.

_____

_____

_____

5. You want to cite Kestutis Zadvydas, Plaintiff, versus John B.Z. Caplinger and Immigration and Naturalization Service, Defendants. This 1997 federal district court case from the Eastern District of Louisiana is published in volume 986, page 1011, of *Federal Supplement*. The Fifth Circuit Court of Appeals reversed the district court in an opinion styled *Kestutis Zadvydas v. Lynne Underdown*. The Fifth Circuit's 1999 opinion is published in volume 185, page 279, of *Federal Reporter*, Third Series.

_____

_____

_____

6. You want to cite Metro Broadcasting, Incorporated, Petitioner, versus Federal Communications Commission, et al. This August 30, 1990, United States Supreme Court case is published in volume 497, page 547, of *United States Reports*; in volume 110, page 2997, of *Supreme Court Reporter*; and in volume 111, page 445, of *Lawyer's Edition*, Second Series. In a decision issued on June 12, 1995, the Supreme Court explicitly overruled *Metro Broadcasting* in *Adarand Constructors, Inc. v. Pena*, published in volume 515, page 200, of *United States Reports*. [*Note: The Federal Communications Commission is commonly referred to by its initials.*]

_____

_____

_____

7. You want to cite Avery Dennison Corporation versus Jerry Sumpton. This 1999 Ninth Circuit Court of Appeals case is published in volume 189, page 868, of *Federal Reporter*, Third Series. The decision reverses the decision of the Central District of California in this case. The Central District's 1998 opinion explains the issues more clearly and thoroughly and is published in volume 999, page 1337, of *Federal Supplement*.

-----

8. You want to cite Lyons Partnership, Plaintiff-Appellant, versus Ted Giannoulas d/b/a The Famous Chicken, Defendant-Appellee. This 1999 federal case from the Fifth Circuit Court of Appeals is published in volume 179, page 384, of *Federal Reporter*, Third Series. This decision affirms the 1998 decision of the United States District Court, Northern District of Texas, in this case. The district court's decision is published as *Jonathan Hart v. Lyons Partnership* in volume 14, page 947, of *Federal Supplement*, Second Series, and contains a much more thorough recitation of the significant facts than the Fifth Circuit's opinion.

-----

9. You want to cite Robert T. Darden versus Nationwide Mutual Insurance Company. This 1992 federal case from the Fourth Circuit Court of Appeals is published in volume 969, page 76, of *Federal Reporter*, Second Series, and affirms the trial court decision of the Eastern District of North Carolina. The Eastern District's 1989 decision is published in volume 717, page 388, of *Federal Supplement*, and gives the best explanation of the issues in this case. The Fourth Circuit was later reversed by the United States Supreme Court in a 1992 decision found in volume 503, page 318, of *United States Reports*.

-----

10.   You want to cite the United States of America versus Anthony Gallagher. This 1979 federal case from the Third Circuit Court of Appeals is published in volume 602, page 1139, of *Federal Reporter*, Second Series. The United States Supreme Court dismissed certiorari of this case on January 17, 1980. This dismissal is published in volume 444, page 1040, of *United States Reports*. The Supreme Court subsequently denied certiorari on January 21, 1980. The denial is published in volume 444, page 1043, of *United States Reports*. Both the dismissal and the denial were related to issues for which you intend to cite the Third Circuit opinion.

_____

_____

_____

Chapter 11

SECONDARY SOURCES

> Before reading this chapter, read Bluepages rules B15, B16, and B18, and main body rules 15-18, including all subsections. Pay special attention to the charts of examples at the beginning of each main body rule.

By now, you are highly proficient in citing any type of case law or legislative enactment. But you may want to cite to information located in other sources such as books, law reviews, and periodicals. You may even find yourself needing to cite to something more esoteric like a letter, a telephone interview, or an unpublished working paper. *The Bluebook* even has rules for citing to sources such as these in their original media. Because you are already proficient in citing sources of positive law, citing these other print sources will be a snap.

However, you may be doing more and more of this type of research over the Internet or through an electronic database. Therefore, this chapter covers citation to both print and electronic sources. Rule 15 governs books and pamphlets; Rule 16, periodical materials; Rule 17, unpublished and forthcoming publications; and Rule 18, electronic sources. Bluepages rules B15-16 and B18 cover the citation of all these sources in legal documents and office memoranda.

A. BOOKS

First, you will notice that Rule 15 requires both the author's name and the title to appear in LARGE AND SMALL CAPITALS. However, B2 provides instead that in legal memoranda and court documents, we italicize the title of books and that authors' names appear in plain type. The basic citation form for a book, however, is the same as shown at the beginning of Rule 15. The basic book citation will contain information regarding:

- the full name of the author or authors,
- the title of the book,
- the editor and/or translator, if any, and
- the date.

If you would like to send your reader to a specific page or pages in the book, the page number would immediately follow the title.

Author, *Title* Pg. (Editor/Translator, Edition, Date).

Rule 15.1 tells you to give the author's name just as it appears. Unlike other citation systems you may have learned in your undergraduate or graduate studies, you do not rewrite the name to put the surname first. If the book has two authors, include both names joined by an ampersand (&) in the order that the names appear in the book.

Jonathan Harr, *A Civil Action* (1997).

Burton Silver & Heather Busch, *Dancing with Cats* (1999).

However, if the book has more than two authors, you may include the name of only the first author immediately followed by the words "et al."

J. Myron Jacobstein et al., *Fundamentals of Legal Research* 121 (6th ed. 1994).

Notice that Rule 15.1(b) tells you that you may list more than two authors by name when the inclusion of other authors is "particularly relevant." Whether an author is particularly relevant depends on whether knowing of the author's participation will help the reader better understand the weight or substance of the source. Fame alone does not make an author "particularly relevant."

The next piece of information that your reader will need after the author is the title of the work. You should include the full title as it appears on the title page. Do not alter the title by abbreviating or omitting words, but capitalize according to Rule 8, which tells you to capitalize all words except articles, conjunctions, and prepositions of four or fewer letters. Rule 8 also tells us to always capitalize the first word in a title and the first word following a colon.

Paul Alexander, *Salinger: A Biography* (1999).

Remember, the overriding concern in legal citation is that the reader should have enough information to find the exact source that you are citing. Therefore, if the book has many editions or translations, you will need to include the editor or translator. The name of an editor will be followed immediately by the abbreviation "ed." and the name of a translator will be followed immediately by the abbreviation "trans." The abbreviations for "editor," "translator," and similar publishing terms appear in T14. If a book has two editors or translators, then both names will appear and be followed immediately by "eds." or "trans." respectively. The naming of editors and translators follows the same rule as the naming of authors; if a book has more than two editors or translators, then you may include the name of only the first editor or translator followed by "et al." Editor and translator information appears in the date parenthetical.

Gabriel Garcia Marquez, *Love in the Time of Cholera* 69-70 (Edith Grossman trans., 1988).

Sometimes, a book will not have a specific author, only an editor. In this situation, no author information will appear, and the editor information will appear in the date parenthetical.

The Antarctic Treaty Regime (Gillian D. Triggs ed., 1987).

The last piece of information you must include is the date of publication. Many books have only one publication date. However, some books are published in several editions, sometimes by the same publisher and sometimes by different publishers. If only one publisher has published a book, then you include only the number of the edition and the year the edition was published in the date parenthetical. (Always cite to the latest edition.) This information is necessary for your reader to be able to consult a source that you are citing by page number. The page numbers of various editions will not be consistent, so your reader will need to know exactly what edition you are citing.

> J. Myron Jacobstein et al., *Fundamentals of Legal Research* 121 (6th ed. 1994).

However, if more than one publisher has published the book, then you must indicate the name of the editor, if any, the name of the publisher, abbreviated according to T6 and T10, and the date of publication of the edition you are citing. If the publisher has published several editions of the work, you will also need to include the edition. You will also include in a separate parenthetical the original date of publication, unless the work is regularly updated or revised. For example, if you are citing a work of literature, you would include in the date parenthetical the name of the publisher and the date of the edition that you are citing. You would also include the original publication date in a separate parenthetical because the actual book is not being updated or revised.

> Thomas Hardy, *Tess of the D'Urbervilles* (David Skelton ed., Penguin Books 1978) (1891).

B. COLLECTIONS

Many books that you will cite will be collections of articles or essays. These sources follow the rule for shorter works in collection, Rule 15.5. In your legal citation, you must include:

- the full name of the author of the specific work that you are citing,
- the title of the specific work,
- the title of the collection,
- the page number on which the specific work appears,
- the editor and translator, if any,
- the numbered edition, if applicable, and
- the date.

> Author, *Work Title*, *in Collection Title* Pg. (Editor/Translator, Edition, Date).

Although Rule 15.5.1 provides that the name of the specific work appears in italics and the name of the collection in large and small capitals, B15 modifies that rule and tells us to italicize the titles of both. The name of the author appears in ordinary roman type, regardless of whether the author wrote all of the works in the collection.

Anthony A. Peacock, *Strange Brew: Tocqueville, Rights, and the Technology of Equality, in Rethinking the Constitution: Perspectives on Canadian Constitutional Reform, Interpretation, and Theory* 122, 125–56 (Anthony A. Peacock ed., 1996).

In addition, some frequently cited books have special citation forms. Rule 15.8 gives you the citation forms for *The Bible*, *The Federalist*, the *Manual for Complex Litigation*, plays written by William Shakespeare, and other frequently cited works.

C. PERIODICALS

You will also on occasion cite to articles in periodicals and law reviews. Rule 16 provides the rules on citing to periodical materials. B16 tells you that the name of the author should appear in ordinary roman type, the title of the article should be italicized, and the title of the publication should appear in ordinary roman type. This instruction overrides the typeface conventions given in Rule 16, which tell you to put titles of periodicals in large and small capitals. The basic form is similar to the form used for shorter works in a collection. In your legal citation, you must include

- the full name of the author of the article that you are citing,
- the title of the article,
- the title of the publication and any other pertinent volume or series information,
- the page number on which the specific work appears, and
- the date.

This information will appear in your legal citation differently depending on whether your source is a "consecutively paginated journal" or a "nonconsecutively paginated journal."

1. Consecutively Paginated Journals

Rule 16.4 governs consecutively paginated journals. The most common consecutively paginated journal you will use is a law review. Law reviews are organized by volumes, which generally correspond to an academic year. However, each "volume" may be printed in separately bound publications with edition numbers. For example, Volume 22 of a certain law review may actually span three separately bound publications, which are usually soft-bound editions. Each publication may be given a number: Volume 22, No. 2. Once a volume is complete, the soft-bound numbered editions are collected and permanently bound as one volume. Therefore, the pages in each publication are numbered beginning with page 1 in Volume 22, No. 1 and ending with the last page of Volume 22, No. 3. Because of this numbering system, only the volume number and the page number are necessary to point your reader to the correct publication.

Author, *Article*, Vol. Periodical Pg. (Date)

Christine Hurt, *The Bluebook at Eighteen: Reflecting and Ratifying Current Trends in Legal Scholarship*, 82 Ind. L.J. 49 (2007).

2. Nonconsecutively Paginated Journals

You may also need to cite to a nonconsecutively paginated journal, such as a magazine. Rule 16.5 governs nonconsecutively paginated journals. The format is generally the same as above, but without a volume designation. Instead, you will include the full date of publication before the page number on which the article cited appears. This information will enable your reader to find a specific issue of a nonconsecutively paginated journal. Note that *The Bluebook* has its own abbreviations for months of the year in T12. The page number follows the word "at."

Author, *Article*, Periodical, Full Date, at Pg.

Lizzie Widdicombe, *Gwyneth's World*, New Yorker, Apr. 25, 2011, at 23.

Notice that you never put the title of the article in quotation marks. Also note that when citing to any periodical, however paginated, you must consult T13, which lists abbreviations for common legal periodicals and for words commonly used in periodical titles, and also T10, which lists abbreviations for geographical regions. Rule 16.4 tells you to use these Tables to abbreviate the title of the cited periodical.

3. Newspapers

The other type of periodical that you may refer to in your legal writing is a newspaper. Rule 16.6 governs newspapers. The format is the same for nonconsecutively paginated journals. If the newspaper article does not name an author, then you simply omit any author information. Again, B16 tells you that the title of the article is italicized, but the title of the periodical and the name of the author appear in plain type.

Author, *Article*, Periodical, Full Date, at Pg.

Michael S. Schmidt & Richard Sandomir, *Baseball Taking Control of Dodgers' Operations*, N.Y. Times, Apr. 21, 2011, at B2.

Rule 16.7 governs the specialized formats for less common sources, such as student-written law review materials, book reviews, newsletters and symposia.

D. NONPRINT & ELECTRONIC SOURCES

On the occasions you will need to cite to a source that is unpublished in a written medium, Rules 17 and 18 cover these types of sources. Some of these sources are addressed in Rule 17 and others, including the Internet, are covered in Rule 18. The charts at the beginning of each rule are valuable references for quickly locating the rules for whichever nonprint or electronic source you wish to cite.

For all sources, *The Bluebook* expresses a strong preference in rules B18, 17, and 18 for citation to a print source. However, if the print source is difficult to obtain, or if no print source exists, you may cite to only a nonprint or electronic source.

Bridget Crawford, *Strawberry Shortcake Gets a Makeover at 30*, Feminist Law Professors (July 12, 2010), http://www.feministlawprofessors.com/2010/07/rainbo/.

B18 also tells you that you may include a parallel citation to an electronic source — either commercial database or Internet URL — if that would improve access. This parallel citation is appended to the print source with a comma.

Helene Cooper, *Bin Laden is Dead, U.S. Official Says*, N.Y. Times, May 2, 2011, at A1, www.nytimes.com/2011/05/02/world/asia/osama-bin-laden-is-killed.html.

As you work through the exercise, use the example charts at the beginning of Rules 15-18 in *The Bluebook* to assist you with the various sources you will be asked to cite. These charts will simplify your work considerably.

Exercise 11
SECONDARY SOURCES

Put the following information in correct *Bluebook* citation form. All sources are being cited in citation sentences. Although this exercise builds on the rules used in the previous exercise, this exercise focuses on Rules 15, 16, and 18 and B15, B16, and B18. You should follow the convention of placing one space after a colon, period, or question mark within a title.

1. "The Nature of the Judicial Process," a book published in 1992 by the Yale University Press in New Haven. The author is Benjamin N. Cardozo. You want to focus your reader's attention on pages 65 through 67.

   _____

   _____

   _____

2. "The New Jim Crow: Mass Incarceration in the Age of Color Blindness," a book by Michelle Alexander, published in 2012 by The New Press.

   _____

   _____

   _____

3. An article by Genevieve B. Tung and Ruth Anne Robbins entitled "Beyond #thenew10 — the Case for a Citizens Currency Advisory Committee," published beginning on page 195 of volume 69 of Rutgers University Law Review in 2016.

   _____

   _____

   _____

4. "Anna Karenina," a novel written by Leo Tolstoy in 1877 and originally published in that year. You are citing to the 1995 edition published in Oxford by Oxford University Press, which is not the original publisher. In this edition, the original text was translated by Louise Maude and Aylmer Maude.

   _____

   _____

   _____

5. "When Justice Lets Us Down," a magazine article by Jim Dwyer, Peter Neufeld, and Barry Scheck, published in the February 14, 2000, issue of *Newsweek*. The article appears on page 59. Assume you are citing this article for a proposition for which the full list of authors' names in not particularly relevant.

_____

_____

_____

6. A newspaper article by James F. Peltz entitled "Dow dives 1,175 points, wiping out 2018 gains." This article appeared at A1 of the *Los Angeles Times* on Tuesday, February 6, 2018.

_____

_____

_____

7. An article by Carrie Sperling and Kimberly Holst entitled "Do Muddy Waters Shift Burdens?" This 2017 article appeared in volume 76 of the Maryland Law Review beginning on page 629. You wish to direct your reader's attention to page 632 of this article.

_____

_____

_____

8. An essay entitled "The Categorical Imperative" by Thomas W. Pogge, which appeared on page 189 of the larger collection "Kant's Groundwork of the Metaphysics of Morals." This work was published in 1998 by Rowman & Littlefield Publishers, Inc. in Lanham, Maryland. You wish to direct your reader's attention to material spanning pages 199 and 201 of this essay. No editor is listed for this collection.

_____

_____

_____

9. "A Gilded Provenance," a magazine article by James Reginato in the December 15, 2017, edition of *Vanity Fair*. This article begins on page 118.

_____

_____

_____

10. You wish to cite to verses 12:1 through 12:6 of the Book of Revelation in *The Bible*.

_____

_____

_____

11. The poem "Her Whole Life is an Epigram" by William Blake, published in a 1994 collection entitled "William Blake" by the Oxford University Press in Oxford. The editor of the collection is Michael Mann. The poem appears on page 115. Assume that this poem is cited the same way as an essay or article in a collection.

_____

_____

_____

12. An article by Susie Salmon entitled "Reconstructing the Voice of Authority." This article was published in 2017 in volume 51 of Akron Law Review on page 143.

_____

_____

_____

13. "NYPD Begins Implicit Bias Training Three After Eric Garner's Death," a post by Chantal Da Silva, published on the Newsweek website on February 6, 2018. This post is accessible online at http://www.newsweek.com/nypd-begins-implicit-bias-training-three-years-after-eric-garners-death-800326.

_____

_____

_____

14. You want to cite to a blog posting by Staci Zaretsky to the blog Above the Law entitled "Be Prepared, Because the SEC is Coming for CryptoLawyers." The post is dated February 6, 2018, at 2:31 p.m.. The post appears at https://abovethelaw.com/2018/02/be-prepared-because-the-sec-is-coming-for-cryptolawyers

_____

_____

_____

15. You wish to cite an episode of More Perfect, a podcast about the Supreme
     Court. The episode is called, "One Nation, Under Money" The podcast was
     produced by WNYC Studios and is dated January 30, 2018. You accessed it at
     https://player.fm/series/radiolab-presents-more-perfect/one-nation-under-
     money.

_____

_____

_____

Chapter 12

PARENTHETICALS

> Before reading the chapter, read Bluepages rules B1.3 and B10.1.5, and main body rules 1.5, 1.6(c), and 10.6.

We know that legal citation serves two primary purposes: to give attribution to a source and to give locating information for a source. In addition, you have probably learned in your legal writing course that citations can also help make your writing more concise. Your citation can minimize or eliminate the need for some detailed explanation. For example, citations can give the year of decision and the jurisdiction of the case so that you do not have to give that information textually.

Instead of:

In 1995, the Texas Supreme Court held that false imprisonment is the willful detention of another without that person's consent and without authority of law. *Randall's Food Mkts., Inc. v. Johnson*, 891 S.W.2d 640 (Tex. 1995).

You can write:

False imprisonment is the willful detention of another without that person's consent and without authority of law. *Randall's Food Mkts., Inc. v. Johnson*, 891 S.W.2d 640 (Tex. 1995).

Citation parentheticals and signals provide additional citation tools for giving your reader useful information without including that information in a detailed discussion. In this chapter, you will learn how to use parentheticals. In the next chapter, you will learn how to use signals, both alone and in conjunction with parentheticals.

You have probably noticed in your legal reading that a great deal of information of several kinds is enclosed in parentheses at the end of some citations. This information falls generally into two categories: weight of authority and explanation. Weight of authority parentheticals give the reader information that indicates the precedential value of a cited case.

Welsh v. United States, 398 U.S. 333 (1970) **(plurality opinion)**.[1]

---

[1] Information appears in bold print for highlighting purposes only. You should not format any part of your citations in bold print.

Explanatory parentheticals provide additional information to make clear to the reader the reason for the citation.

In re Marriage of Wood, 567 N.W.2d 680 (Iowa Ct. App. 1997) **(upholding an order modifying child support and requiring the father to contribute toward college expenses of the children).**

While weight of authority parentheticals are only used with case citations, explanatory parentheticals may be used with any type of authority cited.

A. WEIGHT OF AUTHORITY PARENTHETICALS

Rule 10.6.1 explains how the case's precedential value should be included in a citation. Generally, two types of information indicate that the case does not have the same value as other cases decided by the same court—information that indicates the weight of the authority (*e.g.*, en banc, per curiam, unpublished table decision) and information that shows that the proposition cited is not the clear holding of the majority of the court (*e.g.*, 5-4 decision, dissenting opinion, dictum). For example, a case decided by a single Supreme Court justice sitting as a circuit justice has less precedential value than one decided by the entire Court. In that case, T1.1 (Circuit Justice subsection) gives the format for that parenthetical:

(Scalia, Circuit Justice)

Similarly, a quotation of text from a dissenting opinion would not have the same weight as a quotation from the majority opinion. In that case, the parenthetical would look like this:

TXO Prod. Corp. v. Alliance Res. Corp., 509 U.S. 443, 473 (1993) **(O'Connor, J., dissenting).**

The page numbers given are only those for the initial page of the case and the page for the specific material cited. Those are the only page numbers needed because Rule 3.2(a) tells us *not* to include the initial page number of concurring or dissenting opinions.

In drafting weight of authority parentheticals, be guided by the examples in Rule 10.6.1.

B. EXPLANATORY PARENTHETICALS

Legal writers sometimes include information in explanatory parentheticals to citations to provide additional information that makes clear to the reader the relevance of the citation. Parentheticals provide a clear, concise, economical means of getting the maximum information to the reader with a minimum of detailed explanation. Their use is especially helpful when the writer does not really want to discuss the parenthetical information in text but still considers it necessary to help the reader fit the citation into the overall picture.

Rule 1.5 gives the general rules for the mechanics of including explanatory parentheticals in citations to cases, statutes, and secondary sources. Rule 1.6(c) supplements Rule 1.5 with specific guidance for giving commentary in an explanatory parenthetical. Rule 12.7 gives specific rules for using explanatory parentheticals with statutes. B.11 is a good general guide on when and how to use explanatory parentheticals. The following discussion is applicable to all types of authority.

Most often, explanatory phrases begin with the present participle form of a verb (one that ends in -*ing*).

> W. Wendell Hall, *Standards of Review in Texas*, 29 St. Mary's L.J. 351, 354 (1998) (**explaining** the difference between the standards of review for "no evidence" and "insufficient evidence").

Because the explanation is a phrase, it does not need a period within the parentheses.

Commentary phrases governed by Rule 1.6(c) and 10.6.2 also begin with -*ing* verbs. Commentary explains how the authority cited is related to the authority in the parenthetical.

> La. Civ. Code Ann. arts. 2317, 2322 (West 1979) (**codifying** the rule in *Coulter v. Texaco, Inc.*, 547 F.2d 909, 913 (5th Cir. 1977)).

> *Meeker v. Hamilton Grain Elevator Co.*, 442 N.E.2d 922 (Ill. 1982) (**quoting** *Bonebrake v. Cox*, 499 F.2d 951 (8th Cir. 1974)).

If the context of the citation makes a participial phrase unnecessary, a shorter phrase may be used:

> The interviewer may be anyone authorized to investigate employment matters. *See, e.g., Black v. Kroger Co.*, 527 S.W.2d 794 (Tex. Civ. App.—Houston [14th Dist.] 1975, no writ) (**store manager**); *Safeway Stores, Inc. v. Amburn*, 388 S.W.2d 443 (Tex. Civ. App.—Fort Worth 1965, no writ) (**security guard employed by Safeway**).

C. ORDER OF PARENTHETICALS

Because case citations may include both weight of authority parentheticals and explanatory parentheticals, legal writers need a rule to guide them in ordering multiple parentheticals. Rule 10.6.3 requires that writers list weight of authority parentheticals before explanatory parentheticals and that both follow the court and date parenthetical of the cited case.

> *O'Connor v. Bd. of Educ.*, 449 U.S. 1301, 1306 (1980) (**Stevens, J., concurring**) (**affirming an order vacating a temporary injunction**).

If the citation also includes prior or subsequent history, the parenthetical should follow the court and date parenthetical of the primary cited case rather than following the last case in the citation.

> *Bennett v. Plenert*, 63 F.3d 915 (5th Cir. 1995) (**holding that ranchers and irrigation districts were not within zone of interests protected by ESA**), *rev'd on other grounds*, 520 U.S. 154 (1997).

Mastering the art of drafting explanatory parenthetical phrases will help you become a polished, professional legal writer—one who gets his or her point across in the fewest possible words.[2] With a few well-chosen words in a parenthetical phrase, you will be able to communicate the crux of a case or other authority without discussing it at all in text.

D. DRY RUN

Let's walk through the process of figuring out (1) whether a citation needs a parenthetical and (2) if it does, how to put it together.

Suppose we want to cite *Smith v. Brown*, 123 U.S. 456, 467 (1970). We are citing Justice Euclid's concurring opinion. Concurrences do not have the same precedential value as majority opinions. Accordingly, Rule 10.6.1 indicates that we need a parenthetical phrase because the proposition for which it is cited is "not the single, clear holding of a majority of the court." The examples show that we should convey the appropriate weight of authority by adding the following weight of authority parenthetical after the basic citation:

(Euclid, J., concurring).

Although this is a well-known case, we wish to cite it for one of its lesser-known propositions. Therefore, Rule 1.5 and B10.1.5 recommend an explanatory parenthetical to make the citation's relevance clear.

So we must decide what to say and how to say it in the parenthetical. We are citing page 467 of the case on which Justice Euclid says in dicta that if X were Y, the jury's verdict would not have been allowed to stand. In our brief, we are arguing that the general rule represented by *Smith v. Brown* should not apply to our client's case because, on our facts, X *is* probably Y. How can we word that in an explanatory parenthetical so that it will be clear and concise?

First, the parenthetical phrase should begin with a present participle verb. We cannot use "holding" because the statement was dicta and appeared in a concurring opinion. Instead, we could use "suggesting" for our first word. For the rest, we can simply say "that if X were Y, the jury's verdict would not have been allowed to stand." Although we could quote the court's language in our parenthetical, the better practice is to paraphrase unless the actual words of the court are particularly memorable or concise.

Finally we must decide in what order to put the parenthetical phrases. Rule 10.6.3 guides us here. The weight of authority parenthetical must precede the explanatory parenthetical. So the completed citation would look like this:

Smith v. Brown, 123 U.S. 456, 467 (1970) (Euclid, J., concurring) (suggesting that if X were Y, the jury's verdict would not have been allowed to stand).

Notice the one space between each set of parentheses and the period at the end of the citation sentence *outside* the final parenthesis.

---

[2] For instruction on crafting effective parenthetical phrases, see Michael Smith, Advanced Legal Writing (2d ed. 2008).

Checklist for Parentheticals

- If the case has less precedential value than the court's clear majority opinions, have you included a weight of authority parenthetical that follows the examples in Rule 10.6.1?

- If the relevance of the cited authority is not clear, have you included an explanatory parenthetical that follows the examples in B1.5 and B10.1.5 and Rules 1.5 and 10.6.2?

  - If so, have you used a present participle verb to begin your explanatory or commentary parenthetical? If you did not use a present participle verb, is the context of the explanation clear enough to warrant a shorter phrase?

- If you have both weight of authority and explanatory parentheticals, have you listed the weight of authority parenthetical first?

- If your citation includes prior or subsequent history, have you listed the parenthetical(s) immediately after the court and date parenthetical of the cited authority as shown in Rule 10.6.3?

- Have you left only one space before the opening parenthesis of the parenthetical?

- Have you put the period ending your citation sentence *outside* the final closing parenthesis?

Exercise 12
PARENTHETICALS

Put the following information in correct *Bluebook* citation form. All cases are being cited in citation sentences. Assume that all citations will appear in a brief to a federal court. Although this exercise builds on the rules used in the previous exercises, this exercise focuses on B10.1.6 and B1.3, and Rules 1.5(a)(i), 10.6, and 12.7.

Note: In these problems, the wording for any explanatory phrase will appear in the text of the problem in quotation marks. Changes in wording will be read online as an error. This should not be construed as meaning that explanatory parentheticals have one "right" phrasing. This is simply a limitation imposed by having your work checked online.

1. State of Michigan, Petitioner, versus Raymond and Emma Jean Clifford. This 1984 United States Supreme Court plurality opinion is published in volume 464, page 287, of *United States Reports*; in volume 104, page 641, of *Supreme Court Reporter*; and in volume 78, page 477, of *Lawyer's Edition*, Second Series.

_____

_____

_____

2. Teresa Harris versus Forklift Systems, Incorporated. This 1993 United States Supreme Court opinion is published in volume 510, page 17, of *United States Reports*, and in volume 62, page 4004, of *United States Law Week*. You wish to refer specifically to material appearing on page 25 in the concurring opinion of Justice Ginsburg.

_____

_____

_____

3. Julia H. Tashjian, Secretary of State of Connecticut, Appellant, versus Republican Party of Connecticut, et al. This 1986 United States Supreme Court case is published in volume 479, page 208, of *United States Reports*. Both Justice Stevens and Justice Scalia wrote dissents. You wish to cite from page 235 of Justice Scalia's dissenting opinion "suggesting that if the concept of freedom of association is extended to casual contacts, it will be of no analytical use."

_____

_____

_____

4. In a discussion about the purposes of recent legislative enactments affecting personal relationships, you wish to cite section 11.07.010 of the *Revised Code of Washington*, the official state code of Washington. Legislative intent indicates that the purpose of this statute is "encouraging couples to resolve estate planning questions when terminating their marital relationship." This section appears in the code's 1998 main volume.

---

5. The People of the State of California versus Jennifer Wheeler. This 1992 Supreme Court of California case is published in volume 841, page 938, of *Pacific Reporter*, Second Series, and in volume 14, page 418, of *California Reporter*, Second Series. You want to draw attention particularly to material on page 940 of the opinion "citing" section 1859 of the California Civil Procedure Code, which is part of *West's Annotated California Codes*. This section of the code appears in the 1983 main volume. [*Note: You must properly draft the citation for section 1859 to include in your parenthetical.*]

---

6. In the Matter of Christopher E. Lucas, Respondent. This July 14, 2000, per curiam Supreme Court of Kansas case is published in volume 7, page 1186, of *Pacific Reporter*, Third Series. You wish to cite this case in a discussion about the propriety of sanctions for attorney misconduct and specifically for its "holding that a two-year suspension was appropriate for attorney's misrepresentation that he had closed a client trust account when he continued to use the account."

---

7. John J. Cannon, Plaintiff-Appellant, versus Irving L. Krakowitch, George Clayton, Jr., and E.R. Williams, Defendants-Respondents. This 1959 Superior Court of New Jersey Appellate Division case is published in volume 148, page 213, of *Atlantic Reporter*, Second Series. You want to explain to your reader that the court's holding was in the context of "remanding the matter to the trial court for the assessment of damages by the jury."

---

8. You wish to cite article 37.07 from the 2007 main volume of *Vernon's Texas Code of Criminal Procedure Annotated* "requiring that the State consent to any change in defendant's punishment election." [*Note: The Texas Code of Criminal Procedure, published by West, has not yet been incorporated into Texas' subject matter codes.*]

---

9. In the Matter of The Estate of Svab. This 1966 Court of Appeals of Ohio, Seventh District, case is published in volume 220, page 720, of *North Eastern Reporter*, Second Series. You wish to cite the portion of the opinion on page 723 "recognizing a presumption of undue influence." The Supreme Court of Ohio affirmed this decision in a 1967 opinion published in volume 228, page 609, of *North Eastern Reporter*, Second Series.

---

10. In a discussion of the differences between statutes regulating criminal conduct and those regulating civil rights, you wish to cite Professor Julie Goldscheid's recent article "arguing that the Supreme Court's decision erroneously characterized the VAWA civil rights remedy." This November 2000 article is titled "*United States v. Morrison* and the Civil Rights Remedy of the Violence Against Women Act: A Civil Rights Law Struck Down in the Name of Federalism." It appears in Cornell Law Review, volume 86, page 109.

Chapter 13

SIGNALS

Before reading the chapter, read Bluepages rule B1.2 and main body rules 1.2-1.4, including all subsections.

In the previous chapter, you learned that you can add parenthetical explanations to give your reader helpful information without making that information part of the text of your document. Citation signals are another tool you can use to give valuable information without a detailed explanation.

You have probably noticed citation signals in citations in the legal reading you have done already. Signals can properly be used with any kind of cited authority. The purpose of signals is to show the reader how the authority cited relates to the text it follows and, in some cases, how it relates to other material in the same citation sentence. The eleven signals are divided into four categories of relationship: support, comparison, contradiction, and background.

Support	Comparison	Contradiction	Background
[no signal]	*Compare* . . .	*Contra*	*See generally*
E.g.,	[and] . . .	*But see*	
Accord	*with* . . .	*But cf.*	
See	[and] . . .		
See also			
Cf.			

When you use a signal to describe the relationship between text and citation, a parenthetical explanation can be helpful in elaborating on that relationship. In fact, some relationships will not be clear to the reader without a parenthetical explanation. For that reason, *The Bluebook* often encourages or recommends the use of parentheticals with signals.

No parentheticals	Parentheticals encouraged	Parentheticals strongly recommended
[no signal]	*See also*	*Cf.*
E.g.,	*See generally*	*Compare . . . with . . .*
See		*But cf.*
Accord		
Contra		
But see		

Because the primary purpose of signals is to give the reader information without a detailed textual discussion, writers often take full advantage of signals by using one signal to introduce more than one source. When signals introduce more than one source, the sources are separated by semi-colons and ordered according to Rule 1.4. Rule 1.4 tells us how to order different types of authority in a single citation sentence (*e.g.*, cases and statutes) and also how to order authority of only one type in a single citation sentence (*e.g.*, cases from several jurisdictions). For example, if a citation sentence includes both a case and a journal article, Rule 1.4 instructs that the case (Rule 1.4(d)) should be listed before the article (Rule 1.4(i)).

> *Contra City of Los Angeles v. Lyons*, **461 U.S. 95** (1983); Brandon Garrett, Note, *Standing While Black: Distinguishing Lyons in Racial Profiling Cases*, **100 Colum. L. Rev. 1815** (2000).

On the other hand, if a citation sentence includes only cases, Rule 1.4(d) gives the order of cases within the sentences and also says that cases decided by the same court should be listed in reverse chronological order.

> *See, e.g., Heath v. Jones*, 817 S.W.2d 335 (**Tex. 1991**); *Cooper v. Smith*, 527 S.W.2d 898 (**Tex. 1975**); *Ludwick v. Miller*, 931 S.W.2d 752 (**Tex. App.—Fort Worth 1996**, no writ).

Writers can also maximize the use of signals by using more than one signal in a citation sentence. This is helpful when you want to describe both the relationship of the citations to the text and the relationship of the citations to one another. Rule 1.3 gives three rules for ordering signals:

- Signals should appear in the order listed in Rule 1.2.

> ***Accord** State v. Michaels*, 642 A.2d 1372 (N.J. 1994); ***see also*** *Commonwealth v. Allen*, 665 N.E.2d 105, 108-09 (Mass. App. Ct. 1996).

- Signals of the same type (*e.g.*, support) must appear in a single citation sentence separated by semi-colons (see above example).

- Signals of different types must be in separate citation sentences (study example in Rule 1.3).

As with all other parts of a legal citation, signals have specific typeface rules. Introductory signals in citations are always italicized in court documents and legal memoranda, as provided in B1. Notice that the signals in the examples following Rules 1.2–1.4 are not italicized. You'll recall that this is because the examples in the white pages follow the typeface conventions for scholarly works (law review articles) rather than practitioner documents (memos and briefs). You are to follow the typeface conventions modeled in the Bluepages, not the white pages.

Signals are punctuated according to the list in Rule 1.2. Notice that commas are only used with *e.g.* Notice also that the comma following *e.g.* is not italicized, while a comma within a signal is italicized along with other words in the signal (*See, e.g.,*). This is consistent with a rule you are already familiar with, Rule 2.1(f), which requires that commas within a case name be italicized while the comma following a case name is not. Remember, too, that a citation sentence has the same capitalization rules as a textual sentence: The first word must be capitalized. Therefore, a signal that begins a citation sentence is capitalized; otherwise, the signal is not capitalized.

> ***Accord*** *State v. Michaels*, 642 A.2d 1372 (N.J. 1994); ***see also*** *Commonwealth v. Allen*, 665 N.E.2d 105, 108-09 (Mass. App. Ct. 1996).

Before you begin the exercise, let's go through an example of a citation that uses a signal and a parenthetical.

Suppose we want to cite *Rancher v. Farmer*, 888 P.2d 222 (Mont. 1985), because it is additional source material to the more recent cases we have been discussing in text. *Rancher v. Farmer*, as well as the cases we have discussed, clearly supports the argument we have made. The point for which we are citing the case is that the court held that X is not Y in Montana. The question is, how can we indicate all that without having actually to discuss the case in text? Easy: Introductory signals to the rescue!

First, look at Rule 1.2, the signal rule. Quickly scanning subsection (a) we see that the first four signals listed do not quite describe our situation, but the fifth one, *see also*, looks good. *See also* best describes the relationship between this citation and the text, because we have already discussed several cases that support the textual proposition. We wish to use *Rancher v. Farmer* only as additional source material.

> *See also Rancher v. Farmer*, 888 P.2d 222 (Mont. 1985)

Notice that no comma follows the signal.

Reading further in the description of *see also* in Rule 1.2, we find that the use of a parenthetical explanation with *see also* is encouraged to help the reader understand the relevance of the cited material. How will we write our parenthetical? Remember from the previous chapter and Rule 1.5 that an explanatory parenthetical phrase should begin with a present participle verb, so consider the various *-ing* verbs that spring to mind. Here, what the court *held* is exactly our point and explains the relevance of *Rancher v. Farmer* in the context of our argument. All we have to do, then, is change "held" to "holding" and proceed with the rest of the phrase. So our finished parenthetical will be as follows:

> (holding that X is not Y).

Remember from Rule 10.6.3 that the explanatory parenthetical will follow the court and date element of the basic citation. Our final citation, complete with signal and parenthetical, then, will look like this:

See also Rancher v. Farmer, 888 P.2d 222 (Mont. 1985) (holding that X is not Y).

Remember to put a single space between the court and date parenthetical and the explanatory parenthetical. Also remember that the period at the end of the citation sentence goes outside the parentheses.

And that's all there is to it!

Checklist for Signals

- Does your authority directly state the proposition, identify the source of a quotation, or identify an authority you mentioned in text?

  - If so, you can skip the rest of this checklist because "[no signal]" fills the bill.

  - If not, you must have a signal, so continue.

- Have you selected the appropriate signal from Rule 1.2?

- Have you only included commas in the signal if the signal is or includes *e.g.*?

- Have you italicized the signal?

- If your signal requires commas, have you italicized only those commas that fall within the signal?

- Have you capitalized the signal if it is the first word of your citation sentence?

- Have you left out any commas that are not shown in the examples in Rule 1.2?

- Does the citation need an explanatory parenthetical?

  - If not, you can skip the rest of the items in this checklist because the items following this one deal exclusively with parentheticals.

  - If so, continue through the checklist.

- Have you drafted a brief explanation describing the relevance of the citation?

- Have you selected an appropriate verb to begin your parenthetical explanation?

- Have you put that appropriate verb into *-ing* form?

- Have you put the period that ends the citation sentence outside the final parenthesis?

Exercise 13
SIGNALS

Put the following information in correct Bluebook citation form. All sources are being cited in citation sentences. Although this exercise builds on the rules used in the previous exercises, this exercise focuses on B1.2 and Rules 1.2, 1.3, and 1.4. Determine what, if any, introductory signal you should use and what, if any, parenthetical explanation you should include.

Note: When a rule relating to a signal encourages or recommends a parenthetical explanation, the correct answer on the ICW will include one. Likewise, where the signal rule does not call for an explanatory parenthetical phrase, the correct answer will not include one. As in the Parentheticals exercise, the wording for any needed parenthetical phrase will appear in quotation marks.

1. In a brief to the United States District Court for the Northern District of Texas, you quote directly from Elvis Presley Enterprises, Incorporated, versus Barry Capece and Velvet, Limited. This 1996 Southern District of Texas case is published in volume 950, page 783, of *Federal Supplement*. The material you quoted appears on page 789. Draft the citation that should follow the quote.

   _____

   _____

   _____

2. In a memorandum of law supporting a motion to exclude the testimony of a young child, you write that "psychological studies suggest that children are highly suggestible as witnesses." To present helpful background for this statement, you wish to cite an article by Professors Stephen J. Ceci and Richard D. Friedman "analyzing psychological studies of children and confirming that suggestive interviewing techniques are frequently used successfully with young children." The 2000 article is titled "The Suggestibility of Children: Scientific Research and Legal Implications" and is published in volume 86, page 33, of Cornell Law Review. Draft the citation that should follow your statement.

   _____

   _____

   _____

3. In a brief to the United States District Court, Southern District of Illinois, you write that "a plaintiff in a breach of contract suit benefits from a presumption that the defendant had a duty to act in good faith." Although this proposition is not directly stated in any authority, it can be inferred from a statement in Southwest Whey, Incorporated, versus Nutrition 101, Incorporated, an October 2000 case from the United States District Court, Central District of Illinois. The opinion is published in volume 117, page 770, of *Federal Supplement*, Second Series. Draft the citation that should follow your statement.

_____

_____

_____

4. In a memorandum supporting a Motion to Dismiss Indictment to be filed in a Texas state trial court, you write that "criminal law recognizes that an object may be considered a deadly weapon even when its intended use would not ordinarily cause injury." Although this proposition is not directly stated in any single authority, it can be inferred from many court opinions finding defendants guilty for using non-traditional weapons. Citation to *all* of those cases would not be helpful or necessary, so you have chosen a couple of opinions that will be sufficient to make your point. You have determined that a Texas Court of Criminal Appeals case best illustrates the point. That opinion is David Paul Frost versus The State of Texas, a 2000 case published in volume 25, page 395, of *South Western Reporter*, Third Series. You have further determined that a second case would also be somewhat helpful to illustrate your point. That case is a 1997 Florida District Court of Appeal case styled Dexter Mitchell versus State of Florida. That case is published in volume 698, page 555, of *Southern Reporter*, Second Series. Draft the citation that should follow your statement.

_____

_____

_____

5. In a brief to a Missouri Court of Appeals, you write that "the sale, provision, and installation of electrical equipment is sufficiently goods-intensive that the Uniform Commercial Code applies." Although your research did not find a case directly on point for this proposition, you did find a case "holding that the Uniform Commercial Code applies to a transaction involving the sale, provision, and installation of plumbing equipment." This case is Cork Plumbing Company, Incorporated, versus Martin Bloom Associates, Incorporated, et al., a 1978 Missouri Court of Appeals case published in volume 573, page 947, of *South Western Reporter*, Second Series, and in volume 25, page 1245 of the *UCC Reporter Service*. Although the holding in *Cork Plumbing* is different from the proposition in your brief, it is sufficiently analogous to lend support to your position. Draft the citation that should follow your statement.

_____

_____

_____

6. In a brief to the United States Court of Appeals for the Fourth Circuit, you write that "courts disagree on the standard that should be used to determine landlord liability for injuries caused by dangerous animals living on the premises." You wish to offer support for this proposition by comparing cases from two jurisdictions that use different standards. The first case is James J. Palermo versus Raymond Nails. This 1984 Pennsylvania Superior Court case "holding that the landlord could be liable if landlord was aware of the animal's vicious propensities" is published in volume 483, page 871, of *Atlantic Reporter*, Second Series. The second case is Jessica Lee Ann Mitchell versus Harold Bazzle d/b/a Village Hills Mobile Home Park. This 1991 South Carolina Court of Appeals case "holding that the landlord could not be liable even though landlord knew of vicious propensities of the animal" is published in volume 404, page 910, of *South Eastern Reporter*, Second Series. Draft the citation that should follow your statement.

_____

_____

_____

7. In a brief to the Idaho Supreme Court, you write that "the elements of criminal assault are an unlawful attempt coupled with apparent ability to commit a violent injury on the person of another." These elements come directly from Idaho's criminal assault statute, section 18-901, subsection (a) of the 2007 *West's Idaho Code Annotated* main volume. Draft the citation that should follow your statement.

_____

_____

_____

8. In a brief to the Supreme Court of Indiana, you argue that the owner of a servient estate has the right to determine the location of an easement created by necessity so long as that owner's choice is reasonable. You wish to cite a case from Kentucky that directly states the rule you have asserted. That case is a 1909 Kentucky Court of Appeals case styled M.R. Roland versus G.W. O'Neal and published in volume 122, page 827, of *South Western Reporter*. Although no Indiana cases are directly on point, you wish to further support your argument with an Indiana case that is sufficiently similar to let the reader know that the Kentucky law you have discussed in detail is consistent with the law of Indiana. The Indiana case you wish to cite is a 1903 Indiana Appellate Court case styled Harvey Thomas versus Ellen McCoy and published in volume 66, page 700, of *North Eastern Reporter*. Draft the citation that should follow your argument.

_____

_____

_____

9. In a brief to the Georgia Supreme Court you wish to cite Joseph Roger O'Dell, III, versus J.D. Netherland, Warden, et al. This 1997 United States Supreme Court case is published in volume 521, page 151, of *United States Reports* in volume 117, page 1969, of *Supreme Court Reporter* and in volume 138, page 351, of *Lawyer's Edition*, Second Series. You wish to indicate in your citation that this case constitutes additional source material that supports the same proposition as the case you have discussed in the immediately preceding text. You also want to explain through your citation that the case is relevant because it is "citing" the *Official Georgia Code Annotated*, section 17-8-76 (published in the 1982 main volume). Draft the citation that should follow your text. [*Note: You must properly draft the citation for the statute to include in your parenthetical.*]

_____

_____

_____

10. In a memorandum of law in support of a Motion to Dismiss, you write that "the law does not recognize a cause of action giving relief to public library workers exposed to Internet pornography by the library's patrons." Although your thorough research did not reveal any cases to support such a cause of action and, therefore, you believe this to be an accurate statement of the current law, you wish to disclose to the judge that a law review note takes the contrary position that certain existing causes of action are sufficiently broad to encompass relief for public library workers. This 1999 signed note by student author Kim Houghton is titled "Internet Pornography in the Library" and is published in volume 65, page 827, of the Brooklyn Law Review. Draft the citation that should follow your statement.

_____

_____

_____

Chapter 14

LEGISLATIVE & ADMINISTRATIVE RESOURCES

> Before reading this chapter, read Bluepages rules B12.1.5, B13, and B14, and main body rules 12.4, 13, and 14.

Legislative history and administrative resources can be seen as the bookends bracketing volumes of statutes. Legislative history documents reflect and give insight into the process by which a particular bill either becomes or does not become enacted law. At the other end of the process, the regulatory agencies promulgate regulations that help make the enacted statute operational. The documents generated by regulatory agencies and by the rest of the executive branch of government are collectively referred to as administrative resources. Accordingly, rules governing use and citation of legislative resources begin in Chapter 12, which also covers enacted statutes. Chapter 13 focuses on additional legislative materials, and Chapter 14 contains provisions for citing certain administrative and executive resources. For convenience, this chapter of the *ICW* is divided into two subsections: legislative history resources and administrative resources.

A. LEGISLATIVE RESOURCES

This chapter and the accompanying exercises focus exclusively on federal materials. States vary widely in the publication of legislative materials, but many state legislative materials are patterned generally after the federal model. Therefore, the citation of legislative history follows the same general principles, whether federal or state.

In an increasingly codified legal system, statutory interpretation becomes a vital skill in many areas of legal practice. Often, a legal writer will rely on the intent of the legislature enacting a statute to properly interpret that statute. Legal writers look to the documents that are produced in the legislative process to determine that legislative intent.

To understand how to cite these documents, let's refamiliarize ourselves with the path a bill takes through Congress on its way to becoming "law." As we walk through that progression, we will take side excursions into sections of *The Bluebook* that show how to cite the publications at each step. Let's trace a wholly fictional bill from a Congressman's desk into the pages of the *United States Code*.

In the first session of the 112th Congress, Representative Blue introduces a bill he calls the Excellence in Legal Writing Act of 2011. This bill is the 911th bill introduced into the House of Representatives during this session, so the number given to the bill is H.R. 911. Rule 13.2(a) would govern citation of the **unenacted bill** at this point:

Excellence in Legal Writing Act, H.R. 911, 112th Cong. (2011).

Our bill is referred to the House Committee on Education, which in turn refers it to its subcommittee on Improvement of the Legal Profession, which then conducts hearings. The printed transcript of the hearing held on September 11, 2011 shows on its cover the title "Excellence in Legal Writing Act: Hearing on H.R. 911 Before the Subcommittee on Improvement of the Legal Profession of the House Committee on Education." According to Rule 13.3, we cite to committee hearings by including the title, which should include the bill number and the name of the subcommittee and committee, the number of the Congress, the page number, if any, and the year. If we cite to a particular part of the testimony at the hearings, we include a page number and a final parenthetical statement explaining whose testimony we are citing. B5.1.6 tells us to italicize the title, and we must abbreviate the words in the title according to T6, T9, and T10.

Excellence in Legal Writing Act: Hearings on H.R. 911 Before the Subcomm.
on Improving the Legal Profession of the House Comm. on Educ., 112th
Cong. 27–28 (2011) (statement of Mary Smith, law student).

After hearings, the committee votes to recommend passage of our bill. The committee submits the bill, as amended, in a committee report. Committee reports are good sources of legislative history, including changes to the language of the bill and an explanation of the reasons behind the committee's recommendation. Committee reports are numbered sequentially. A citation to a report, according to Rule 13.4(a), will include the name of the house, the number of the Congress and the number of the report, a page number, and a year of publication. B5.1.6 tells us that the citation should appear in plain roman type. If the House report on our bill is the 83rd report this session, a cite to page 5 of the report would look like this:

H.R. Rep. No. 112-83, at 5 (2011).

For some but not all bills, House and Senate reports, as well as recent conference reports, are reprinted, together with the related bill, in the *United States Code Congressional and Administrative News* (abbreviated U.S.C.C.A.N. and informally called "you–scan"). When a legislative resource is available in U.S.C.C.A.N., you should give a parallel cite to it, as provided in Rule 13.4(a).[1] Our committee report is one of the documents reprinted in the permanent 2011 edition of that publication beginning at page 6144:

H.R. Rep. No. 112-83, at 5 (2011), *reprinted in* 2011 U.S.C.C.A.N. 6144.

---

[1] When citing to a report reprinted in U.S.C.C.A.N., *The Bluebook* gives two conflicting examples. In Rule 13.1, the U.S.C.C.A.N. information is added to a citation with the words "*reprinted in*." In an example under Rule 13.5, the U.S.C.C.A.N. information follows the words "*as reprinted in*." For purposes of consistency, the ICW will use the rule given in 13.1.

Now, back to our bill! Our bill now goes to the floor of the House for a vote. The bill is debated on the floor of the House, and the *Congressional Record* includes a transcript of the debate. The *Congressional Record* is published daily during each legislative session. At the end of each session, all daily editions are published in a permanent, bound edition. The rule governing citation to the debate is Rule 13.5. If the debate is published on page 23,251 of volume 143 of the permanent edition of the *Congressional Record*, our citation would look like this:

143 Cong. Rec. 23,251 (2011).

If we were citing the debate before the permanent edition of that volume of the *Congressional Record* became available, Rule 13.5 tells us that we would cite to the daily edition. That means that we would give the full date, remembering to abbreviate the month as shown in T12, and that information would become part of the parenthetical. Notice that an "H" precedes the page number in the daily edition citation because the daily editions are separated into House and Senate proceedings, each with its own consecutive pagination. The page numbers in the separate volumes are preceded by either an "H" or an "S" so we will know which section of the daily edition, House or Senate, to consult:

143 Cong. Rec. H12,345 (daily ed. Apr. 14, 2011).[2]

Notice that in the two preceding citation examples, a comma appears in the page numbers. Rule 6.2(a) tells us that when a number has five digits or more, we must separate it into groups of three digits by comma.[3]

Our bill passes the House! After approval by the House of Representatives, the bill is sent to the Senate for consideration. The Senate will have similar committee hearings and debates on our bill. Once the Senate also passes it, it is assigned a session law number. Most federal session laws are called Public Laws, and Public Law numbers reflect simply the number of the Congress, here the 112th, and the chronological order of the enactment. The law we are tracing is the 205th law enacted by the 112th Congress; therefore, its session law number is Public Law 112-205, abbreviated "Pub. L." as shown in Rule 12.4. We also include the year of passage of the bill in a date parenthetical. The session law citation is as follows:

Excellence in Legal Writing Act, **Pub. L. No. 112-205** (2011).

Federal session laws are compiled in *United States Statutes at Large*, which, as T1.1 indicates, is abbreviated "Stat." Our newly enacted statute appears on page 683 of volume 127 of *United States Statutes at Large*. When the statute appears in that source, its citation will include that information:

Excellence in Legal Writing Act, Pub. L. No. 112-205, **127 Stat. 683** (2011).

---

[2] On Lexis and Westlaw, all *Congressional Record* cite page numbers are preceded by "H" or "S" even after the document is printed in the permanent edition. However, your citations should follow the Bluebook rule of eliminating the "H" or "S" once it is published in the permanent edition.

[3] However, the Eighteenth Edition of *The Bluebook* deleted an example from Rule 6.2(a) that showed a comma being used with a daily edition page reference: "H17,326." Perhaps the legislative history of Rule 6.2(a) suggests that a comma should not be used with a daily edition page reference. Until this mystery is resolved, the *ICW* will follow the text of Rule 6.2(a) and require a comma.

Notice that Rule 12.4(e) also tells us to omit the date parenthetical if the year is part of the name of the statute. If the year of enactment were part of the title of this statute, the citation would look like this:

> Excellence in Legal Writing Act of 2011, Pub. L. No. 112-205, 127 Stat. 683.

When you know where the enacted statute will be codified (usually this information is part of the enacted bill itself), include that information parenthetically in its citation, as Rule 12.4(f) provides. Thus if our statute will be codified as section 1331 of title 53 of the *United States Code*, its citation will reflect this information:

> Excellence in Legal Writing Act, Pub. L. No. 112-205, 127 Stat. 683 **(2011) (to be codified at 53 U.S.C. § 1331).**

Once the act is codified, you will ordinarily cite it as a statute according to the provisions of Chapter 12. However, occasionally you may have a specific reason to cite the bill or the session law. For example, you may wish to cite to the session law when it is codified in many scattered sections or titles of the official code, as provided in Rule 12.2.2(a). In addition, you would also want to cite to the original bill to show amendments and to document legislative history, as provided in 13.2(b).

Much of the time you will research and compile the legislative history of a statute that applies to your case yourself. Some particularly important federal acts, however, are the subjects of separately bound legislative histories. They would be cited according to the same rules as those governing citation of books and other nonperiodic materials, Rule 15 of *The Bluebook*. You will learn more about the sources of already compiled legislative histories in your research course. Among other valuable lessons, you will learn that if a legislative history has already been compiled, you will save valuable research time if you use it rather than re-inventing that particular wheel.

B. ADMINISTRATIVE RESOURCES

Just as enacted statutes are positive law, so are the administrative rules and regulations that implement them. Administrative regulations originate with the agencies and departments of the executive branch of government. Take a couple of minutes now to scan the provisions of Rule 14 and familiarize yourself with its contents. You will see that, as in other areas of *The Bluebook*, the coverage is briefly described in Rule 14, and Rule 14.1 demonstrates the basic citation forms of administrative and executive materials. New T1.2 now covers citations to materials from federal agencies, including the Executive Office of the President, as well as specialized provisions relating to federal tax and SEC (Securities and Exchange Commission) materials, areas outside the scope of this exercise.

The primary sources of federal administrative materials are the *Code of Federal Regulations* and the *Federal Register*. Rule 14.2(a) governs final rules and regulations published in the C.F.R., and Rule 14.2(b) deals with proposed rules and regulations found in the daily editions of the *Federal Register*, as well as administrative notices of numerous kinds.

The C.F.R. is the official compilation of codified rules and regulations and is organized and cited much like the *United States Code*. Both are arranged topically into titles; however, the titles of the U.S.C. and the C.F.R. do not parallel one another. Otherwise, the citation forms are also quite similar. If a rule or regulation has a familiar name, then you should include the name. Just as the title number precedes the abbreviation U.S.C., so the title number of the regulation precedes the abbreviation C.F.R. And just as the section number of the statute follows the code abbreviation, so the regulation section or part number follows its code abbreviation. Also like statutory citations, a citation to a regulation needs a date. This date is the date on the relevant volume of the C.F.R., not the date of adoption of the rule or regulation.

statute: Employee Retirement Income Security Act of 1974, 29 U.S.C. § 1132 (2006).

regulation: Employee Welfare Benefit Plan, 25 C.F.R. 2510.3-1 (2011).

Rule 14.2(a) tells us to cite final rules to the *Code of Federal Regulations* if possible, or to the *Federal Register* if not, indicating parenthetically where the new rule will be codified. (If all this sounds familiar to you, aren't you glad you learned the federal statutory citation material so well?) Each title of the *Code of Federal Regulations* is revised each year, but not all at the same time. The revisions are spread out over four quarterly publication dates, January, April, July, and October. The date of each volume of *Code of Federal Regulations* appears on the cover.

As you have learned (or soon will learn) in legal research, when an administrative agency proposes (or promulgates) a regulation, notice of that proposed regulation is published in the *Federal Register*. When a regulation is adopted in its final form, it will appear first in the *Federal Register* and then in the *Code of Federal Regulations*. The *Federal Register* contains administrative notices, proposed regulations, and other announcements. Rule 14.2(b) tells us to cite notices of a proposed regulation the same way we would cite a final regulation, except that we must add the date of proposal to the normal date parenthetical.

Incentive-Based Compensation Arrangements, 76 Fed. Reg. 21,170 (Apr. 14, 2011).

If you cite only a part of a rule, as with a pinpoint citation to any source you must indicate in the full citation not only the beginning page of the rule, but also the specific page on which the cited material appears. The following pinpoint citation to a final rule demonstrates this:

Grants to Combat Violent Crimes Against Women on Campuses, 64 Fed. Reg. 39,774, 39,777 (1999) (to be codified at 28 C.F.R. pt. 90).

Where the relevance for the pinpoint citation is not obvious to the reader, Rule 1.5 on parenthetical information recommends an explanatory parenthetical.

Grants to Combat Violent Crimes Against Women on Campuses, 64 Fed. Reg. 39,774, 39,777 (1999) (to be codified at 28 C.F.R. pt. 90) (responding to a comment that the regulation was "too heavily oriented toward directing victims to the criminal justice system").

When an agency schedules a public hearing or a meeting or makes a public announcement, the *Federal Register* publishes the official notice.

Open Meeting Notice, 64 Fed. Reg. 51,755 (1999).

Although most of the administrative materials you will have occasion to cite in law school and in your law practice will probably be of the regulatory type, presidential proclamations, and executive orders are also administrative materials, and we cite them according to T1.2. Proclamations and executive orders that are currently in force are published in the C.F.R. If not in the C.F.R. you may cite to the *Federal Register*. Some presidential documents are also reprinted in the statutory codes. If the document has been reprinted in the statutory code, give a parallel cite to the *United States Code*; if the document does not appear in the *United States Code* but does appear in one of the unofficial codes, *United States Code Annotated* (U.S.C.A.) or *United States Code Service* (U.S.C.S.), then use the unofficial code for the parallel citation.

Exec. Order No. 12,781, 3 C.F.R. 373 (1992), *reprinted in* 3 U.S.C.A. § 301 app. at 878–79 (West 1997).

Remember to check T1.1 for the proper citation form for the unofficial code you are using.

Notice that the citation above is to a *page* number in the *Code of Federal Regulations*, not a *section* number. Because Presidential documents are not rules, they have no section numbers. T1.2 Executive Orders, Presidential Proclamations, and Reorganization Plans sends us back to 14.2, where we learn that "in certain circumstances" we are to cite to page numbers rather than section or part numbers in the *Code of Federal Regulations*. Presidential papers constitute "certain circumstances" for the purpose of Rule 14.2.

Short forms for regulatory citations are discussed in Rule 14.4, which closely parallels the statutory short forms set forth in Rule 12.10. For example, if you had already given a full citation for the following final rule:

Regulations Governing Off-the-Record Communications, 18 C.F.R. § 385 (2011).

then as Rule 14.4(c) and B5.2 provide, a later citation to the same section after intervening cites would take the following form:

18 C.F.R. § 385.

or

§ 385.

C. ELECTRONIC SOURCES

Both state and federal governments have been proactive in using the Internet to make accessible the documents generated by law makers in the process of enacting and enforcing law. For that reason, you often have the option of including a parallel citation to one of the documents you've just learned how to cite. This will improve access to the document for your reader. Parallel Internet citations to for these documents are appended just as they are with cases, statutes, and secondary sources. You simply append the URL to the print source citation using a comma.

H.R. Rep. No. 104-83, at 5 (1999), reprinted in 1999 U.S.C.C.A.N. 6144, http://thomas.loc.gov.

Employee Retirement Income Security Act of 1974, 29 C.F.R. § 2510.3-1 (1999), http://www.dol.gov/dol/allcfr/Title_29/Part_2510/29CFR2510.3-1.htm.

See how easy it all is? Take it away, citation wizards!

Exercise 14
LEGISLATIVE RESOURCES

A. LEGISLATIVE RESOURCES

Put the following information in correct *Bluebook* citation form. All sources are being cited in citation sentences in a brief to be filed in a federal court of appeals. Although this exercise builds on the rules used in the previous exercises, this exercise focuses on B12.1.1, and B13 and Rules 13 and 12.4.

1. You want to cite to some background information given on page 9 of a committee report from the Committee on Veterans' Affairs of the Senates. This report, number 111-175, accompanies Senate bill number 1237. The bill and the committee report have the same title, Homeless Veterans and Other Veterans Health Care Authority Act of 2010. The bill was introduced in the Senate on June 11, 2009, and the committee report was dated April 9, 2010. This report was not reprinted in U.S.C.C.A.N.

2. You wish to cite a session law called Stem Cell Therapeutic and Research Reauthorization Act of 2015, published in volume 129 of the United State Statutes at Large, at page 2216. The bill was the 104th bill Passed by both houses of Congress in December of 2015 during the 114th Congress.

3. You are writing a memo to a supervising attorney about pending legislation affecting the mental health and wellbeing of law enforcement officers. You want to cite a bill that has been introduced in the Senate during the 115th Congress and give the number 867. Sen. Joe Donnelly introduced the bill on April 6, 2017, which calls for education of mental health professionals about the culture of law enforcement agencies.

4. You wish to cite to a May 4, 2017, House committee report on H.R. 1809 (The Juvenile Justice Reform Act of 2017). The report was given a House report number of 115-111. The report was not published in U.S.C.C.A.N.

5. You wish to cite to a statement of Rep. Carolyn Maloney that was an extension of remarks made when re-introducing the Firearm Risk Protection Act on the floor of the House of Representatives on Thursday, March 23, 2017. The entire testimony is available only in the daily edition of the Congressional Record, volume 163, page E373.

---

6. You wish to cite to a statement of Rep. Mac Thornberry made on the floor of the House of Representatives on May 13, 2015, during the House debate on H.R. 1735, called the National Defense Authorization Act for Fiscal Year 2016. The statement is found in the permanent edition of the Congressional Record, volume 163, page 5534.

---

7. You wish to cite a joint resolution that has the House number 109. The resolution was introduced on July 19, 2017, in the 115th Congress and proposes a balanced budget amendment for the Constitution of the United States.

---

8. In a discussion of the legislative history of the Protecting Academic Freedom in Higher Education Act, you cite to a 2011 report from the House of Representatives Committee on Education and the Workforce. This report was the 177th report in the 112th Congress. You want to cite to information on page 5 of the report.

B. ADMINISTRATIVE RESOURCES

Put the following information in correct *Bluebook* citation form. All sources are being cited in citation sentences in a brief to be filed in a federal court of appeals. While this exercise builds on the rules used in previous exercises, this exercise focuses on Rule 14 and T1.2 Federal Administrative and Executive Materials.

1. In your brief you are citing a rule concerning the registry for visual arts incorporated into a building. The rule is found in title 37 of the Code of Federal Regulations, at section 201.25. The current volume of title 37 was published in July 2018.

   _____

   _____

2. You want to cite a regulation of the Department of Health and Human Services that appears in the current (2018) volume 42 of the Code of Federal Regulations as section 2.22.

   _____

   _____

3. You are citing a proposed rule of the Internal Revenue Service published on February 26, 2018, in volume 83 of the *Federal Register*, beginning at page 8173. The title of the rule is Health Insurance Providers Fee. The proposed rule has not yet been transferred to the Code of Federal Regulations but would be codified at 26 C.F.R. part 57.

   _____

   _____

4. You need to cite to a proposed rule from the U.S. Fish and Wildlife Service published on February 2, 2018, in volume 83 of the *Federal Register*, beginning at page 4,964. The title of the rule is Migratory Bird Hunting; Proposed Frameworks for Migratory Bird Hunting Regulations. The proposed rule has not yet been transferred to the Code of Federal Regulations but would be codified at 50 C.F.R. part 20.

   _____

   _____

5. You need to cite to a final rule of the Coast Guard published on February 15, 2018, in volume 83 of the *Federal Register*, beginning at page 6,795. The title of the rule is Drawbridge Operation Regulation, Hampton River, Hampton, NH. The rule has not yet been transferred to the Code of Federal Regulations but would be codified at 33 C.F.R. part 117.

   _____

   _____

6.   Draft a citation for Executive Order No. 13,822, signed on January 9, 2018, by President Donald J. Trump. This order was published on January 12, 2018, and is found in volume 83 of the *Federal Register* at page 1513. This executive order does not appear in the *Code of Federal Regulations* or the *United States Code*.

_____

_____

7.   7. Draft a citation for Presidential Proclamation No. 9688, signed on December 29, 2017, by President Donald J. Trump. This proclamation was published on January 4, 2018, in the *Federal Register*, volume 83, page 587. This proclamation does not appear in the *Code of Federal Regulations* or the *United States Code*.

_____

_____

Chapter 15

WHEN DO I CITE?

> Before reading this chapter, read Bluepages rule B1.1.

We have often found that in teaching our students the intricacies of legal citation rules, we need to stop and focus on the most important citation rule: The rule that tells us when we must cite! Knowing when to cite can be tricky until you have some experience in writing legal memoranda, court documents, or a scholarly paper. You probably have brought some citation placement experience with you from your undergraduate or graduate work. For better or worse, legal writing requires very precise and usually frequent citation of the propositions in our legal writing—probably more precision and frequency than writing in other fields.

Citation placement requires that you make two decisions: whether a citation is needed and, if so, where to place that citation.

A. WHEN DO I CITE?

The decision of whether or not to include a citation is more important than it might seem. Providing a citation when one is needed (called "attribution") serves two functions. First, attribution strengthens your analysis by demonstrating that you are following the law. Second, attribution helps your reader locate the source you have cited. This is important because legal writing is competitive writing. Both your opponent and the judge will want to read your sources themselves to determine whether your use of the source supports your argument in the way you claim it does. In that way, providing a citation for each source you rely on makes your writing more user friendly.

In addition, attribution in legal writing — as in every other type of writing — is the way to avoid plagiarism, i.e., the passing off of another's ideas as your own. Plagiarism in law school can have far-reaching consequences, including delay or prevention of receiving your license to practice law. Therefore, learning when you need a citation is critical to your success.

The general rule of thumb for legal memoranda and court documents is that you need a citation for every fact, thought, or opinion that comes from another source (not you or your facts). You need a citation even if you are not quoting. The purpose of your citation is to enable your reader to go to a specific page of a specific source and find support for the sentence preceding the citation. If you are detailing the facts of a case or the holding of a case, then you need a citation to that case, whether you are quoting or paraphrasing. If you are quoting or paraphrasing a statute or regulation, then you need a citation. If you are making a proposition about the state of the law generally, then you need a citation to a source that supports that proposition. If you are providing your reader with a rule that you have synthesized from several sources, then you need cites to those sources. Here are some examples of the types of sentences you will write in a legal memorandum or a court document that would need citations:

> In our jurisdiction, courts look to numerous factors when determining whether an individual can establish ownership by adverse possession. *Belotti v. Bickhardt*, 127 N.E. 239 (N.Y. 1920).

> The Court of Appeals of New York held that the defendant's possession must be hostile and under a claim of right; the possession must be actual; the possession must be "open and notorious"; the possession must be exclusive; and the possession must be continuous for a period of twenty years. *Belotti v. Bickhardt*, 127 N.E. 239, 241 (N.Y. 1920).

> The defendant used and rented all portions of a building, a portion of which was built on property owned by the plaintiff. *Belotti v. Bickhardt*, 127 N.E. 239, 240 (N.Y. 1920).

However, you do not need a citation when detailing your own facts or even applying a previously cited rule to your facts. If in doubt, ask yourself: "If my reader turns to this page of this source, would the reader find support for this statement?" Here are some examples to illustrate:

> Tina Trespasser, our client, should be able to show that she meets all five of the requirements to prove adverse possession.

> Tina, like the defendant in *Belotti*, has continuously occupied the land in question and earned income from it.

Notice that some of the examples in this chapter cite to the first page of the case only, while others pinpoint the location of specific material cited. When authority is used to represent a rule of law (*e.g.*, a landmark decision like *Roe v. Wade* for the right to privacy), then the citation does not necessarily require a pinpoint. However, when your citation follows facts or reasoning from the case, a pinpoint citation is needed to help your reader find the information cited.

B. WHERE DO I PLACE THE CITATION?

Citations take two forms: citation sentences and citation clauses. A citation sentence is a citation that you place at the conclusion of a textual sentence. Like every other sentence, it starts with a capital letter and ends with a period.

> The elements of negligence are duty, breach, causation, and harm. *Tortfeasor v. Victim*, 123 St. Rptr. 456 (St. Sup. Ct. 2014).

The textual sentence begins with "The elements of . . ." and ends at the period after "harm." The citation sentence begins with "Tortfeasor . . ." and ends with the period after the end parenthesis. By attributing the textual sentence with a citation sentence, you are telling the reader that all of the information from the preceding textual sentence ("The elements of . . .") came from the source in the citation sentence ("Tortfeasor . . .").

If only a portion of your textual sentence is supported by your source, you may use a citation clause instead.

> The elements of negligence are duty, breach, causation, and harm, *Tortfeasor v. Victim*, 123 St. Rptr. 456 (St. Sup. Ct. 2014), and are satisfied in Ms. Brown's case.

In this situation, the citation is included within the textual sentence and is set off with a pair of commas. You can use a citation clause when your textual sentence is a mixture of both law and fact, and also when your textual sentence is a mixture of legal principles that each come from different sources.

Now that you know how to cite, when to cite, and where to cite, you're all set!

Exercise 15
WHEN DO I CITE?

For this exercise, you will use a set of facts about a fictitious client and two actual cases. You will be given sentences taken in order from a hypothetical discussion section in a legal memorandum. You will need to decide whether each sentence requires a citation to one of the given cases.

If you determine that the sentence *does not* require a citation, then simply leave the space after the sentence blank. (If you are doing this exercise on the website, then type "no citation" in the solution box blank and click "Submit.") If you determine that the sentence does require a citation, then simply type either "Randall's" or "Safeway" in plain type (and without a period) as applicable.

This exercise emphasizes the placement, rather than the form, of citation. Accordingly, when a citation is required, you should type "Randall's" or "Safeway" regardless of whether a full citation, "*id.*," or abbreviated short form ought to be used and regardless of whether a pinpoint cite ought to be included.

> Facts: Your client is Mary Ratchet, a psychiatric nurse. She is employed by Charter Canyon Psychiatric Hospital. On June 14, 2013, the head psychiatrist, Dr. Sam Wright, called her into the staff break room. He then accused her of alcohol abuse and refused to let her leave the locked unit until he was finished talking with her. After the end of the meeting, she left the hospital and has since filed a suit for false imprisonment against Dr. Wright.
>
> Case: *Randall's Food Mkts., Inc. v. Davis*, 891 S.W.2d 640 (Tex. 1995). This is the seminal Texas Supreme Court opinion that states the three elements of false imprisonment. This case does not focus on the element of "detention without authority of law." The facts appear on page 640, and the rule and holding appear on page 642.
>
> *Safeway Stores, Inc. v. Amburn*, 388 S.W.2d 443 (Tex. App. — Fort Worth 1965, no writ). This case focuses on the element of "detention without authority of law." The court specifies what types of employer-employee meetings are lawful. The facts appear on page 443, and the rule and holding appear on page 444.

1. In Texas, the plaintiff in a successful cause of action for false imprisonment must prove three elements: (1) the detention was willful; (2) the detention was without consent; and (3) the detention was without authority of law.

_____

_____

2. In our case, the parties do not dispute that the detention was without Ms. Ratchet's consent or that the detention was willful; however, the parties do disagree about whether the detention was without authority of law.

_____

_____

3. To prove that an employee has been detained without authority of law, we will have to show that the employer was acting outside of the employment relationship by detaining an employee in an inappropriate confrontation unrelated to her duties.

_____

_____

4. Dr. Wright clearly detained Ms. Ratchet without authority of law.

_____

_____

5. In Texas, an employer has "authority of law" to require a discussion with an employee regarding that employee's duties, but that discussion must take place at a logical, proper location and must be conducted in a logical, proper manner.

_____

_____

6. In *Safeway Stores, Inc. v. Amburn*, the Court of Appeals held that an employer was acting within his authority when questioning plaintiff Kenneth Amburn, a cashier, about a possible cash register theft.

_____

_____

7. The court held that discussions regarding employee loyalty are proper, as are discussions held in the only available private space of a business, in this case, the back room of a grocery store.

_____

_____

8. The events of June 14 are very different from the events discussed in *Safeway Stores*.

_____

_____

9. Although both Dr. Wright and Ms. Ratchet have offices, Dr. Wright chose to detain her in the employee break room.

_____

_____

10. In addition, Dr. Wright wanted to speak with her concerning possible alcohol abuse not directly related to her work performance.

_____

_____

Chapter 16

COURT DOCUMENTS: TRIAL & APPELLATE

> Before reading this chapter, read Bluepages rules B17, including all subsections.

So far, we've focused on how to cite authority. However, the law isn't the only material that comes from external sources. The facts also come from external sources. And just as legal readers use the citations in your document to locate and verify the authority you've cited, legal readers also need citations to locate and verify the facts and allegations to which you apply the law in your analysis. Those facts are recorded in a variety of court documents, and those court documents compose what's called the "record" of the case. To fully understand what the record is, you need to first know how documents make their way into the record. Although specific practices vary from jurisdiction to jurisdiction, the general practice of accumulating the record is similar across the country. This chapter will use civil actions in federal courts for illustration.

The first document filed in a case is, of course, the complaint. When a document is "filed," that means it has been submitted to the clerk's office for that court. The clerk's office will start a file for that case and assign it a number. That number is called the "docket number." From that point forward, all documents filed in that case should have that number printed on them, and all documents will be placed in that file in chronological order behind the complaint. Therefore, the next document in the file behind the complaint will likely be some responsive pleading by the defendant. After the initial pleadings in the case, discovery documents (such as interrogatories) and a variety of motions and responses will be filed as they are submitted in the case.

A. CITING DOCUMENTS DURING THE TRIAL PROCESS

While the case makes its way through the trial process, the parties may want to refer back to documents already filed. For example, a Motion for Summary Judgment might refer back to allegations in the Complaint. When the allegations from the Complaint are referenced, the writer will need to cite the Complaint.

The first part of a court document citation is the abbreviated name of the document. For guidance in forming abbreviations for court documents, use BT1 at the conclusion of the Bluepages rules. BT1 contains abbreviations for words commonly found in court document titles. BT1 also instructs you to omit articles and prepositions from any title. Although BT1 does not guide you on whether to abbreviate ordinals (first, second, third, etc.), one of the primary goals of citation is to make the citation as short as possible while still conveying as much information as possible. In that spirit, then, abbreviate ordinals in document names just as you do for reporter and court abbreviations (1st, 2d, 3d, etc.).

> Defendant's Brief in Support of Motion for Summary Judgment
> becomes:
> Def.'s Br. Supp. Mot. Summ. J.
>
> Plaintiff's Motion to Compel
> becomes:
> Pl.'s Mot. Compel

For affidavits and depositions, identify the documents by the affiant's or deponent's surname and the abbreviation for the document.

> (St. James Dep. 37, May 10, 2010.)

> (Wells Aff. ¶ 12.)

The second part of the court document citation is the specific location of the material cited. B17.1.2 encourages as much specificity as possible.

cited by para. number	(Doc. Name ¶ X.)
cited by pg. number	(Doc. Name X.)
cited by line number	(Doc Name pgX:lineX.)
cited by item number	(Doc. Name # X.)

The third part of a court document citation is the date, when needed for clarity. If a party has given more than one deposition or affidavit, identify the document by date as well.

> (Wells Aff. ¶ 12, July 14, 2005.)

Similarly, if many of the same type of documents have been filed (*e.g.*, Motion to Compel, Motion to Quash), specifying the date of the document may help to prevent reader confusion.

Finally, notice that citations to court documents, unlike citations to authority, are enclosed in parentheses. Even though the citation is enclosed in parentheses, it is still considered a citation sentence, and the period is placed just inside the closing parenthesis. However, if the record cite is in a citation clause, it will not contain a period.

> Dr. Carter admits that his treatment plan was unorthodox (Answer ¶ 12) but denies that it was negligent (Carter Dep. 73).

B17.2 tells you that you should use a short form after the first full cite to a court document. Although B17.2 does not give specific rules for shortening court document cites, the examples suggest two common sense solutions: (1) omit dates from short forms, and (2) drop elements of the document name.

Essentially, any short form that sufficiently identifies a lengthy document name would be acceptable.

> *full form:* (Def.'s Br. Supp. Mot. Summ. J. 39.)
> *short form:* (Def.'s Br. Supp. 45.)

Additionally, rule 4.1 does say that "'*Id.*' may be used in citation sentences and clauses for any kind of authority." Just as with other cites to factual, rather than legal, authority, the citation should be inside parentheses.

> (*Id.*)

B. CITING DOCUMENTS ON APPEAL

When an appellate court considers a case, it may have access to three different types of factual information: the record, the transcript of testimony, and exhibits offered at trial.

When a case begins the appellate process, documents filed with the trial court clerk's office are referred to as part of the record ("R.") rather than as individual documents (*e.g.*, "Pl.'s Mot. Compel"). The documents in the clerk's file are consecutively numbered, beginning with the complaint and ending with the last document in the case. At that point, all material is referenced by page number rather than paragraph number. As B17.1.2 points out, it is customary to use "at" when citing to a page number in an appellate record. Therefore, the Complaint might have been cited like this during the course of the trial:

> (Compl. ¶ 3.)

However, when the parties refer to the Complaint in the appellate briefs, it would be cited like this:

> (R. at 1.)

The transcript of trial testimony may be cited as "Trial Tr." and specific material within a transcript may be referred to by page number.

> (Trial Tr. 39.)

The exhibits admitted during trial are cited as "Ex." and bear the abbreviation of the party that offered the exhibit and the number of the exhibit.

> (Def.'s Ex. 12.)

And there you have it! For the record, you're ready for the exercise.

Exercise 16
COURT DOCUMENTS: TRIAL & APPELLATE

Put the following information in correct *Bluebook* citation form. All sources are being cited in citation sentences in a brief to a federal district court. This exercise focuses on B17. You will also need to refer to BT1 for abbreviations of words commonly used in court document titles. Follow the convention of enclosing citations in parentheses, according to the B17.1.1 Bluepages Tip.

1. In a Motion for Summary Judgment, you wish to cite the third paragraph of the First Amended Complaint, filed by the plaintiff. No other party has filed a complaint in this action.

    _____

    _____

2. Without any intervening cites, you again want to cite to the third paragraph of Plaintiff's First Amended Complaint.

    _____

    _____

3. In the same Motion for Summary Judgment mentioned in Problem 1, you wish to cite to numbered paragraph twelve of the two-page affidavit of Miranda J. Hillard, M.D., Ph.D.

    _____

    _____

4. In a Motion to Compel Discovery, you wish to cite to page 3 of Defendant's Interrogatories requesting information from the Plaintiff

    _____

    _____

5. You wish to cite to page 47 of the deposition testimony of Albert Walker

    _____

    _____

6. In an appellate brief, you wish to cite to paragraph 3 of the Court's Verdict. In the consecutively-numbered record compiled by the court clerk, the verdict is on page 392.

    _____

    _____

7. In the next sentence of the same appellate brief and without any intervening cites, you wish to cite again to the same paragraph 3 of the Court's Verdict.

    _____

    _____

8. In an appellate brief, you wish to cite to Defendant's Exhibit 26. No continuously paginated record was compiled for this appeal.

_____

_____

Chapter 17

LAW REVIEW FOOTNOTES

INTRODUCTION

The first sixteen chapters have taught you how to construct citations to be used in office memoranda and legal documents. As a practicing attorney, the vast majority of the writing you will do will be in one of these two categories. However, as a law student writing seminar papers and short articles for law journals, you will need to learn the citation form that is used for citations in scholarly legal writing. This third category of writing encompasses various forms of writing that are found in academic journals: notes, comments, book reviews and full-length articles. Most law school seminar papers are also required to follow this format, as well as most articles found in bar journals and other legal publications.

If you have written extensively in an undergraduate or graduate program, you know that each academic discipline follows citations rules, as to both substance and form, found in publication manuals for that discipline. For example, many liberal arts graduate programs require research papers to conform to the *MLA Handbook for Writers of Research Papers* (the "MLA"), and social science programs commonly adopt the *Publication Manual of the American Psychological Association* (the "APA"). In law schools, most upper-level writing requirements are satisfied by an academic paper whose citations conform to the *Bluebook*, and most law-related academic publications require article submissions to conform to the *Bluebook* as well.

As mentioned before, the *Bluebook* has slightly different rules, mostly typeface conventions, for citations that appear in court documents and legal memoranda and for those that appear in scholarly articles. Therefore, this chapter will enable you to construct academic citations, which we will refer to loosely as "law review citations," from the knowledge you have gained using the preceding chapters of the ICW. Although the other chapters of this book have prepared you for the kinds of writing you have done in a first-year legal research and writing course or in an internship at a law office or other type of legal employment, this chapter will teach you the skills necessary to participate in a journal writing competition, write a seminar paper and prepare a note or comment for a law school journal.

A. CITATION PLACEMENT

One major difference between citations in legal documents and memoranda and law review citations is that law review citations are never embedded in the text; law review citations appear in footnotes, signaled by a superscript numeral, called a "footnote call number," after the clause or sentence that requires the citation (Rule

1.1(a)). The footnote call number appears after most punctuation marks, but before colons and dashes (Rule 1.1(a)). The citation sentence then appears in the footnote itself. Nonetheless, law review citations are still full sentences that begin with a capital letter and end with a period (Rule 1.1(b)(i)).

The footnote may also contain textual sentences that add to the discussion but would distract from the substance of the main text. When these footnote sentences require citation to authority, that authority may be cited in either a stand-alone citation sentence or a citation clause in the same footnote, depending on whether the entire footnote sentence or only a part requires citation (Rule 11(b)).

Minor changes in the Eighteenth Edition include numbering changes,[41] additional examples,[42] and references to new courts, such as the Foreign Intelligence Surveillance Act Court.[43]

---

[41] For example, Rule 3, Volumes, Parts, and Supplements, has been renumbered. The text of former Rule 3.1(a) is now just unnumbered text. Therefore, the former Rule 3.1(b) is now subsection (a) and so on. THE BLUEBOOK: A UNIFORM SYSTEM OF CITATION R. 3, at 58 (Columbia Law Review Ass'n et al. eds., 18th ed. 2005) [hereinafter EIGHTEENTH EDITION].

[42] Some new examples are inserted to help clear up confusion, others to reflect amendments to the rule, and others just to reflect the currentness of the new edition. *See, e.g.*, *id.* R. 12.2.2(b), at 103 (adding an example citing to the Sarbanes-Oxley Act of 2002).

[43] *See id.* R. 10.4(a), at 89 (including a citation form for the Foreign Intelligence Surveillance Court and the Court of Review).

Unlike in the days of typewriters when creating footnotes entailed much planning and a little math, creating footnotes using a word processing program is incredibly simple and much more helpful than endnotes. In WordPerfect, you "Insert" a "Footnote." In Word, you "Insert" a "Reference," then "Footnote." At least one notable legal commentator has suggested using footnotes in all types of legal documents,[1] particularly documents submitted to courts, but so far footnotes are not widely used in law practice.

B.   TYPEFACE CONVENTIONS

In the preceding chapters, we have introduced you to the rules found in the main pages of the *Bluebook*, but also taught you that the parallel rules in the Bluepages, for practitioners, control when the rules differ. For constructing law review citations, however, follow only the rules in the main pages. The first difference you will notice is that in law review citations, parts of citations may be in plain type, ITALICS, or *Large and Small Capitals* (Rule 2.1). Large and small capitals are easily produced using your word processing software: in both Word and WordPerfect, this function is called "small caps" under the "Font" heading. In addition to adding the small caps typeface

---

[1] *See* BRYAN A. GARNER, THE WINNING BRIEF 139–47 (2d ed. 2004).

to statute citations and secondary source citations, law review citations also change the typeface conventions you have learned in certain types of citations, such as case names.

1. Case Names

For full and short citations of cases in legal documents and memoranda, you italicized the case name. However, in law review citations, the case name is not italicized when using the full citation form, only the short form (Rule 2.1(a)).

Therefore,

United States v. Grass, 239 F. Supp. 2d 535 (M.D. Pa. 2003).

becomes

United States v. Grass, 239 F. Supp. 2d 535 (M.D. Pa. 2003).

The acceptable short forms for this case would be identical under the law review citations rules as under the rules for legal documents and memoranda. For example,

Grass, 239 F. Supp. 2d at 546.

or

Id. at 546.

2. Statutes

For legal documents and memoranda, you produced the name of the statutory compilation in plain type, whether the statute was found in the *United States Code* or a state publication, such as the *California Corporations Code*. However, in law review citations, the name of the statutory compilation appears in small caps (Rule 12.3).

Therefore,

Tex. Penal Code Ann. § 12.32(a) (West 2007).

becomes

TEX. PENAL CODE ANN. § 12.32(a) (West 2007).

Because the abbreviation for the *United States Code* is all capital letters, "U.S.C.," the difference in typeface from plain type to small caps is irrelevant.

Note that if you wanted to give the name of a particular statutory act or provision, then that name would still appear in plain type.

This typeface change also applies to specialized statutes covered by Rule 12, such as rules of evidence and procedure (Rule 12.9.3) and model codes, restatements, and sentencing guidelines (Rule 12.9.5).

Therefore,

Fed. R. Civ. P. 31.

becomes

FED. R. CIV. P. 31.

Again, because citations to the statutory tax provisions found in the Internal Revenue Code (Rule 12.9.1) use the all-capital abbreviation "I.R.C.," this typeface change is irrelevant.

3. Legislative, Administrative and Executive Materials

The differences in typeface between legal documents and scholarly articles are less focused with regard to the various types of legislative materials. The law review citation format for legislative bills and resolutions are the same as for legal documents, as well as citations to the *Federal Register* and the *Code of Federal Regulations*. In addition, citations to executive orders and presidential papers remain in plain type. However, for federal reports from the House of Representatives and the Senate, part of the citation is in small caps (Rule 13.4). In addition, citations to the *Congressional Record* abbreviate the title of that publication using small caps (Rule 13.5).

Therefore,

H.R. Rep. No. 104-83 (1999).

becomes

H.R. REP. NO. 104-83 (1999).

and

143 Cong. Rec. H12,345 (daily ed. Apr. 14, 1999).

becomes

143 CONG. REC. H12,345 (daily ed. Apr. 14, 1999).

4. Secondary Sources

In writing seminar papers and other academic articles, you will cite to many more secondary sources than you have previously in writing memoranda, appellate briefs and court motions for your other classes. When practitioners write to each other and to the court, they are attempting to explain what the current state of the law is, citing to primary authority such as statutes and cases. Only when the law does not fully contemplate the situation at hand do practitioners and courts then turn to persuasive authority such as law review articles, treatises and books. However, scholarly writers, who are commonly arguing for a change in an existing legal paradigm, cite to secondary authority frequently. Perhaps understandably, the law review citation form for these types of sources differs from the citation form used in legal documents.

Both the author (Rule 15.1) and title (Rule 15.3) of a book appear in small caps. The names of editors, translators (Rule 15.2) and publishers (Rule 15.4) remain in plain type.

Therefore,

Frederick Lewis Allen, *Only Yesterday* (1931).

becomes

Frederick Lewis Allen, Only Yesterday (1931).

Shorter works such as articles and works in a collection still appear with the author's name in plain type and the title of the work in italics, but the name of the collection or periodical appears in small caps.

Therefore,

Lisa M. Fairfax, *Martha Stewart and Director Independence, in Martha Stewart's Legal Troubles* 359 (Joan MacLeod Heminway ed., 2007).

becomes

Lisa M. Fairfax, *Martha Stewart and Director Independence, in* Martha Stewart's Legal Troubles 359 (Joan MacLeod Heminway ed., 2007).

and

Ann Althouse, *Why a Narrowly Defined Legal Scholarship Blog Is Not What I Want: An Argument in Pseudo-blog Form*, 84 Wash. U. L. Rev. 1221 (2006).

becomes

Ann Althouse, *Why a Narrowly Defined Legal Scholarship Blog Is Not What I Want: An Argument in Pseudo-blog Form*, 84 Wash. U. L. Rev. 1221 (2006).

Finally,

Kristen Hays, *No Fanfare as Skilling Steps into Prison Life*, Hous. Chron., Dec. 14, 2006, at A1.

becomes

Kristen Hays, *No Fanfare as Skilling Steps into Prison Life*, Hous. Chron., Dec. 14, 2006, at A1.

5. Electronic Sources

The core of an electronic source citation is borrowed from the citation form for the underlying source. For example, an electronic source citation for a case contains the same typeface conventions as a case citation, and so does a statute citation, etc. Therefore, when creating an electronic source citation in a law review footnote, review the typeface conventions for the underlying source and consult Rule 18.

Tex. Penal Code Ann. § 12.32(a) (West, LEXIS through 2008 Sess.).

Table 18.1 Typeface Differences

	Legal Memoranda or Document	Scholarly Article
case	*Rutherford v. Chrysler Motors Corp.*, 231 N.W.2d 413 (Mich. Ct. App. 1975).	Rutherford v. Chrysler Motors Corp., 231 N.W.2d 413 (Mich. Ct. App. 1975).
case short form	*Rutherford*, 231 N.W.2d at 415.	*Rutherford*, 231 N.W.2d at 415.
statute	Ariz. Rev. Stat. § 17-454 (2007).	ARIZ. REV. STAT. § 17-454 (2007).
statute short form	Ariz. Rev. Stat. § 17-455.	ARIZ. REV. STAT. § 17-455.
rule	Model Rules of Prof'l Conduct R. 8.4(d) (2003).	MODEL RULES OF PROF'L CONDUCT R. 8.4(d) (2003).
article	William J. Stuntz, *The Pathological Politics of the Criminal Law*, 100 Mich. L. Rev. 505 (2001).	William J. Stuntz, *The Pathological Politics of the Criminal Law*, 100 MICH. L. REV. 505 (2001).
newspaper	John Kass, *Governor Has One Choice Left*, Chi. Trib., Dec. 9, 2008, at A7.	John Kass, *Governor Has One Choice Left*, CHI. TRIB., Dec. 9, 2008, at A7.
book	Henry G. Manne, *Insider Trading and the Stock Market* (1966).	HENRY G. MANNE, INSIDER TRADING AND THE STOCK MARKET (1966).
congressional report	H.R. Rep. No. 110-210, at 23 (2007).	H.R. REP. NO. 110-210, at 23 (2007).
congressional debate	154 Cong. Rec. 10,793 (2008).	154 CONG. REC. 10,793 (2008).
electronic source	*United States v. Bajakajian*, 524 U.S. 321 (1998), *available at* http://supct.law.cornell.edu/supct/cases/name.htm.	United States v. Bajakajian, 524 U.S. 321 (1998), *available at* http://supct.law.cornell.edu/supct/cases/name.htm.
direct citation to electronic source	Sarah Hepola, *My Big, Fat, Unpaid Credit Card Bill*, Salon.com, Jan. 30, 2008, http://salon.com/mwt/feature/2008/01/30/credit_card_debt/.	Sarah Hepola, *My Big, Fat, Unpaid Credit Card Bill*, SALON.COM, Jan. 30, 2008, http://salon.com/mwt/feature/2008/01/30/credit_card_debt/.

C. PARALLEL CITATIONS

In earlier chapters, you learned to construct parallel citations for state cases if required by the local rules. In these parallel citations, readers would be referred not only to a West regional reporter, but also to an official state reporter or a public domain citation. In scholarly writing, however, the audience is intended to be national, even international. Therefore, local rules are irrelevant and scholarly works generally do not contain parallel citations. For state cases in your article or note, merely cite to a regional reporter unless told otherwise by a particular legal publication.

D. SIGNALS AND PARENTHETICALS

When writing for your first-year legal writing class, you probably used a few signals in the court documents and legal memoranda you prepared. Because you were using mostly primary authority, you probably used *"see," "see also"* and *"but see"* more than any others and may have used few of those signals. However, once you begin writing academic papers that make arguments about what the law should be, and not just what the law is, then you may begin to cite to secondary sources that require a signal to reflect the relationship between your assertion and the substance of the cited source. In addition, you will probably be using more parentheticals to assist you in showing your reader the relevance of a particular secondary source. If you become an editor for a law journal, or have an article edited by a law journal, you will find that many journals have their own policies regarding signals, parentheticals and even the types of gerunds that may appear in a parenthetical. The *ICW* has earlier chapters on the use of signals and parentheticals, and those rules apply with even more force to academic writing. Please review those chapters if you would like help in using signals or constructing parentheticals.

E. SHORT FORM REFERENCES AND INTERNAL REFERENCES

In previous chapters, we've discussed the use of *"id."* to reference both cases and statutes that have been cited in the same general discussion in legal documents. Rule 4.1 tells us that *"id."* may be used to cite "any kind of authority except internal cross-references." Therefore, we can use *"id."* to refer to books, articles, legislative history and other types of sources if that source appears in the immediately preceding citation within the same footnote or in the previous footnote, when the previous footnote contains only one source.

We have also discussed how to create a short form for books and cases for situations in which you want to formulate a short form for a source that has been cited previously, but not in the immediately preceding citation. Previous chapters have not discussed short forms for other sources, such as secondary sources, that are commonly cited in scholarly works. For these situations, Rule 4.2 tells us to use *"supra"* and "hereinafter" "to refer to legislative hearings; books; pamphlets; reports; unpublished materials; nonprint resources; periodicals; services; treaties and international agreements; regulations, directives, and decisions of intergovernmental organizations; and internal cross- references" but not for "cases, statutes, constitutions, legislative materials (other than hearings), restatements, model codes, or regulations."

1. Cases and Statutes

When referring to a source cited in the immediately preceding citation, you may still use *"id."* in your law review footnote. Rule 4.1 tells us that "[i]n law review footnotes, use *"id."* when citing the immediately preceding authority within the same footnote or within the immediately preceding footnote *when the preceding footnote contains only one authority."*

If you cannot use *"id."* and must compose an acceptable short form, then Rules 10.9 (Cases) and 12.10 (Statutes) provide the forms for law review citations. Although the short forms are generally the same, note that both Rules 10.9 and 12.10 provide an additional limitation on the use of short forms in academic writings with footnotes, which may be much longer than legal memoranda and may discuss various topics. In these types of writings, you may use a short form to clearly identify a case or statute that "is already cited in the *same footnote"* or "is cited (in either full or short form, including *"id.")* in *a manner such that it can be readily found in one of the preceding five footnotes."*

The purpose of this rule is to enable a reader to easily find a full citation either on the same page that the reader is reading text or on the page or so before it. Given that law review articles have grown so long that some law reviews have begun imposing word limits of 30,000 or fewer on submissions, this rule can save a reader from having to thumb through pages and pages of text in search of a full citation. Therefore, if you have not referred to a case or statute in the previous five footnotes, you will have to provide your reader with a full citation for that source again.

2. Secondary Sources, *"Supra,"* and "Hereinafter"

Again, you may still use *"id."* in citation footnotes to refer to any type of secondary source, such as a book or periodical article, when the source was cited in the immediately preceding citation. However, if you cannot use *"id.,"* then you must refer to the previous secondary source citation using the *"supra"* format as a short form citation (Rule 4.2(a)). This type of short form generally refers to the source by using the author's last name and a reference back to the numbered footnote in which the full citation appears. The citation will also include any type of pinpoint information. The typeface for the author's name will match the typeface used in the original full citation. If the source is a journal article, then the author's name will appear in plain type both in the full citation and the supra short form. However, if the source is a book, then the author's name will appear in small caps in both footnote citations. If the work has more than one author, then use all the authors' names in the supra short form if all authors' names were used in the original citation.

Author, *supra* note X, at Y.

or, if a book

AUTHOR, *supra* note X, at Y.

A comma separates the author's name from the word "supra" in italics, then the word "note" appears in plain type and then the footnote number. Any pinpoint will appear at the end, preceded by a comma and, if the pinpoint is to a page number, the word "at" (Rules 3.2 and 3.3).

³ JAMES D. COX & THOMAS LEE HAZEN, CORPORATIONS (2003).

⁴ *See* Larry E. Ribstein, *Fraud on a Noisy Market*, 10 LEWIS & CLARK L. REV. 137 (2006).

⁵ *See* COX & HAZEN, *supra* note 3, at 420 (explaining the difference between a direct, individual suit and a derivative action).

⁶ *Id.* at 421.

⁷ *See* Ribstein, *supra* note 4, at 155 (noting also that if the market is "noisy" or irrational, damages are even more difficult to attribute to disclosures of fraud).

If the work has no author, then the *supra* form should refer to first piece of information in the citation, usually the title.

⁴³ TORTS STORIES (Robert L. Rabin & Stephen D. Sugarman, eds., 2003).

⁴⁴ United States v. Carroll Towing Co., 159 F.2d 169 (2d Cir. 1947).

⁴⁵ TORTS STORIES, *supra* note 43.

If in your paper you cite to more than one source by a particular author or author group, you must devise a system for distinguishing *supra* forms for the various works. When the two sources appear in the same footnote, distinguishing the sources by something other than footnote number is mandatory for the *supra* short form to work. However, even when two sources by the same author appear in different numbered footnotes, creating a nickname for the sources can also aid your reader. The *Bluebook* does not specifically address the second problem, but the "hereinafter" device can work well in both situations (Rule 4.2(b)). Formulate a shorthand title for each work and use "hereinafter" to label the works as such. In the original citation to the source, at the end of the citation but before any explanatory parenthetical, insert within brackets the word "hereinafter" and the chosen nickname. The words in the nickname appear in the same typeface used for those words in the original citation. The word "hereinafter" appears in plain type.

Then, in subsequent *supra* short forms, use that abbreviated title in connection with the author's name. The hereinafter nickname should appear in the same typeface as whichever part of the full citation it is abbreviating.

⁴ Larry E. Ribstein, *Fraud on a Noisy Market*, 10 LEWIS & CLARK L. REV. 137 (2006) [hereinafter Ribstein, *Noisy Market*].

⁵ *See* COX & HAZEN, *supra* note 3, at 420 (explaining the difference between a direct, individual suit and a derivative action).

⁶ *Id.* at 421.

⁷ *See* Ribstein, *Noisy Market*, *supra* note 4, at 155 (noting also that if the market is "noisy" or irrational, then damages are even more difficult to attribute to disclosures of fraud).

"Hereinafter" is also a useful tool when a normal *supra* short form would be long or cumbersome, for example, when a source has no author but a lengthy title, such as hearings, regulatory filings and various types of reports. Creating a shorthand nickname for a source can also be useful when the source is well known by a particular name.

[18] ATTORNEY GENERAL'S COMMISSION ON PORNOGRAPHY, FINAL REPORT (1986) [hereinafter MEESE REPORT].

[19] *Unlawful Internet Gambling Funding Prohibition Act and the Internet Gambling Licensing and Regulation Commission Act: Hearing on H.R. 21 and H.R. 1223 Before the Subcomm. on Crime, Terrorism, and Homeland Security of the H. Comm. on the Judiciary*, 108th Cong. 8-12 (2003) [hereinafter 2003 Hearing].

[20] NATIONAL GAMBLING IMPACT STUDY COMM'N, FINAL REPORT (1999) [hereinafter "NGISC REPORT"].

[21] *See* MEESE REPORT, *supra* note 18, at 5.

3. Internal Cross-References

Because most legal documents you have written so far have been fairly short, you may not have needed to refer in your text either to a prior discussion or a future discussion within the same writing. In lengthy academic writing, referring to another portion of the same article is quite common, for example, when you want to mention a possible area of concern that you intend to cover in greater detail later in the same article. To alert your reader that you realize this assertion requires authority and that further discussion will satisfy that requirement, you can simply create a footnote that cites to that section of the article, whether it is a textual section or a footnote or group of footnotes. If the cited section appears prior to your textual sentence, use "*supra*," if after, use "*infra*" (Rule 3.5). The portion of the article to which you are referring appears in plain type, with no commas.

> The impact of the appearance of a competitor can be examined by analyzing changes from the Seventeenth Edition to the Eighteenth Edition, particularly the revamping of the Practitioners' Notes into the new "Bluepages."[34] This type of citation archeology has also shown that new editions of the Bluebook have responded to criticisms of earlier editions.[35]

---

[34] *See infra* Part III.B.

[35] *See supra* notes 13-15 and accompanying text.

Although this type of cross-reference can be useful and save writers from repeating themselves, writers can be tempted to insert too many cross-references. Although there are no hard and fast rules, be aware if you are repeatedly referring to sections that appear later in your paper. Your paper could benefit from being reorganized if you are concerned that your reader will not understand one section without referring to a later section. On the other hand, you may merely be inserting unnecessary cross-references.

F.   NEW TYPES OF SOURCES

One thing you will note in writing your first seminar paper or law journal piece is that you will be citing from a more varied set of sources. Although the *ICW* has taught you how to cite to the most frequently cited sources, such as cases, statutes, constitutions, regulations, books and law review articles, you will occasionally need to cite to a source and not know where to begin in formulating a citation form. The best place to begin with the *Bluebook* is with the 37-page index, which is fairly thorough, if not exhaustive. A quick glance at the "B" entries reveals entries for *Ballentine's Law Dictionary*, *Black's Law Dictionary*, blogs, BNA publications, broadcasts, and books and pamphlets such as ABA publications, ALI publications, the Declaration of Independence and government agency reports.

Of course, no matter how often the *Bluebook* is updated or how thorough the index is, every paper will have a source that does not seem to match exactly to a current *Bluebook* rule. When this happens, use your judgment and find a rule that addresses a source similar to the source you need to cite and adapt the citation format.

For example, imagine that you are writing a paper on legal issues arising in space law, particularly in abandoned space equipment orbiting the earth. You want to make the assertion that space law is a growing field and want to cite to a three-day conference at a well known law school as evidence of that assertion. The conference does not have a website at the time of your writing, but you do have a "Save the Date" postcard from the law school announcing the upcoming conference. Consulting the index, you see there are no entries for "postcard," "brochure," "press release," "invitation" or "announcement." However, you notice there are rules for "pamphlets," "leaflets," and "letters." The rule that seems like it might work is Rule 17.2.3 for letters, memoranda and press releases. So, you try to adapt the format something like this, using the date you received the mailing:

> Announcement, Elite College of Law, Join Us at the Third Annual Space Law Conference, March 3-5, 2010 (Jan. 10, 2009) (on file with author).

Good luck!

Exercise 17
LAW REVIEW FOOTNOTES

For this set of exercises, you will revisit citation forms that you know: cases, statutes, legislative and administrative sources, and secondary sources. You know the basic format of sources under *Bluebook* Rules 10–18, but now you will also use the typeface conventions found in the main rules.

For these exercises, you are assumed to know how to form full citations for various types of sources. When in doubt, consult the index to the *Bluebook*. For purposes of these exercises, create the citation that would go into a footnote in an academic article following the typeface conventions and rules for the main pages of the *Bluebook*. All sources are being cited in citation sentences. Although most footnote citations in academic articles begin with some sort of signal, for purposes of these exercises, do not include a signal unless one is provided for you.

Note: When using the large and small caps emphasis, please highlight *as a single unit* the text you want to appear in large and small caps rather than highlighting each word individually. For example, in the citation "123 Harv. L. Rev. 456", you should highlight "Harv. L. Rev." as a single unit and then click on the large and small caps button. Do not include text that does not belong in large and small caps, such as "123" and "456".

CASE CITATIONS

1. Robert Shannon versus Union Pacific Railway Company, a case from the Supreme Court of Kansas, decided February 11, 1888, and reported at volume 16, page 836, of *Pacific Reporter*.

2. The Brotherhood of American Yeomen, defendant-appellant, versus Mrs. Mina Graves, plaintiff-appellee, a case decided by the Court of Appeals of Kentucky, which was the highest state court in that state until 1976. This particular case was decided April 29, 1930, and reported at volume 27, page 670, of *South Western Reporter*, Second Series.

3. The United States of America versus Eddie Wayne Roberson, a case from the United States Court of Appeals, Fifth Circuit, decided April 28, 1989, and reported at volume 872, page 597, of *Federal Reporter*, Second Series.

---

4. Rothman Realty Corp. versus Barton Bereck and Debra Bereck, his wife, a case from the Superior Court of New Jersey, Appellate Division, decided March 17, 1976, and reported at volume 355, page 201, of *Atlantic Reporter*, Second Series.

---

5. Sally Beauty Company, Inc. versus Nexxus Products Company, Inc., a case decided by the United States Court of Appeals for the Seventh Circuit on September 26, 1986, and reported at volume 801, page 1001, of *Federal Reporter*, Second Series.

---

6. Karen Derby versus The Connecticut Light and Power Company, a case from the Supreme Court of Connecticut, decided August 20, 1974, and reported at volume 355, page 244, of *Atlantic Reporter*, Second Series.

---

7. Harland Macia, III, d/b/a Catamount Software, versus Microsoft Corporation, Intuit, Inc., and Meca Software, LLC, a case from the United States District Court of the District of Vermont, decided on June 21, 2001, and reported at volume 152, page 535, of *Federal Supplement*, Second Series.

---

8. Southern California Edison Company versus Public Utilities Commission, a
    case decided by the California Court of Appeal, Second District, Division 3, on
    December 29, 2000, and reported at volume 85, page 1086, of *California
    Appellate Reports*, Fourth Series.

_____

_____

_____

9. Food Lion, Incorporated versus United Food and Commercial Workers
    International Union, et al. and United Steelworkers of America, et al., a case
    decided by the United States Court of Appeals in the District of Columbia on
    January 10, 1997, after oral arguments on November 21, 1996. The case is
    reported at volume 103, page 1007, of *Federal Reporter*, Third Series.

_____

_____

_____

10. Vivienne Rabidue, Plaintiff, versus Osceola Refining Company, Defendant, a
    case decided by the United States Court of Appeals for the Fifth Circuit on
    November 13, 1986, and reported at volume 805, page 611, of *Federal
    Reporter*, Second Series.

_____

_____

_____

STATE AND FEDERAL STATUTES

1. Rule 804(a) of the current Federal Rules of Evidence, published in 2012 in title
    28 of the *United States Code*.

_____

_____

2. Section 911 of title 2 of the *Delaware Code Annotated*, published by
    LexisNexis. This section appears in the 2001 main volume.

_____

_____

_____

3. Subsections 231v(a) through (c) of title 45 of the current *United States Code*, published in 2006. These subsections appear in their entirety in the 2013 Supplement I.

_____

_____

_____

4. Sections 10-9-18 of *West's New Mexico Statutes Annotated*. Part of this citation appears in the 1995 main volume, and part appears in the 2015 cumulative supplement.

_____

_____

_____

5. In a discussion of the current version of certain federal tax law provisions, cite section 2036(a) of the Internal Revenue Code, title 26 of the current *United States Code*, published in 2012. Use the special citation form for tax law provisions.

_____

_____

_____

6. Section 10-3A-24(a)(4) of the *Code of Alabama, 1975*, published by West. This provision appears in the main volume published in 1999. No amendments to this section appear in any supplement or pocket part.

_____

_____

_____

7. Section 413.120(4) of *Michie's Kentucky Revised Statutes Annotated*, published by LexisNexis. The entire text of this subsection appears in the 2015 supplement.

_____

_____

_____

8. Rule 4(a) of the current Federal Rules of Appellate Procedure, published in 2012 in title 28 of the *United States Code*.

_____

_____

_____

9.   Section 4303.33, subsections (A) and (C) of *Page's Ohio Revised Code Annotated*, published by LexisNexis. Both of these subsections appear in their entirety in the 2003 main volume.

_____

_____

_____

10.   Section 1332(a)(2) of title 28 of the current *United States Code*, all of which is printed in the main volume published in 2012.

_____

_____

_____

LEGISLATIVE AND EXECUTIVE SOURCES

1.   You wish to cite to Executive Order No. 13268, issued by President George W. Bush on July 2, 2002, terminating the national emergency declared on July 4, 1999 with respect to the Taliban. This order appears in volume 67 of the *Federal Register* on page 44,751. It is not published in the *Code of Federal Regulations*.

_____

_____

_____

2.   You wish to cite a statement of Sen. Russell Feingold that was made on the floor of the Senate on July 10, 2001, on the death penalty. The transcript of this debate is found in the permanent edition of the *Congressional Record*, volume 147, page 7418.

_____

_____

_____

3.   In a discussion of the legislative history of the Truth in Lending Act, you cite a session law called the Truth in Lending Class Action Relief Act, published in volume 109 of United States *Statutes at Large* at page 161. The law was codified as section 1640 of title 15 of the *United States Code*. The bill was passed in April of 1995 and given the public law number 104-12.

_____

_____

_____

4. You want to use the definition of the term "federal mandate" that appears on page 6 of report number 104-1 of the Senate Committee on Governmental Affairs on Senate Bill 1. The report was published in 1995 and was reprinted in the 1995 volume of the *United States Code Congressional and Administrative News* beginning at page 4; the precise language you are quoting appears on page 10 of that publication.

_____

_____

_____

5. In a discussion on the legislative history of certain laws passed following the attacks on the World Trade Center and the Pentagon on September 11, 2001, you wish to cite a session law called the Uniting and Strengthening America by Providing Appropriate Tools Required to Intercept and Obstruct Terrorism (USA Patriot Act) Act of 2001, published in volume 115 of the *United States Statutes at Large* at page 272. The bill was the 56th bill passed by both houses of Congress in October of 2001 during the 107th Congress. This act is known as the "USA Patriot Act."

_____

_____

_____

6. Draft a citation for the regulations implementing the National Voting Registration Act, 42 U.S.C § 1973gg-1 (1994). The regulations are found in title 11 of the 2008 edition of the *Code of Federal Regulations*, sections 8.3 through 8.6.

_____

_____

_____

7. You wish to cite to a joint resolution that has the Senate number 96. The resolution was introduced and published in 1999 in the 106th Congress under the title "Y2K Act." Assume the resolution was not enacted and that the name of the resolution is relevant.

_____

_____

_____

8. You wish to cite to a May 15, 2001, committee report on H.R. 73 (H. Con. Res. 73). The report was given a House report number of 107-40. The report was not published in U.S.C.C.A.N.

_____

_____

_____

9. You are writing on the history of OSHA, and you want to cite to Executive Order No. 12196, signed by President James E. Carter on February 26, 1980. This order is found at 1980 U.S.C.C.A.N. 7696 and in volume 45 of the *Federal Register*, page 12769. It is not published in the *Code of Federal Regulations* (C.F.R.).

_____

_____

_____

10. You want to cite a regulation of the National Labor Relations Board that appears in the current (2013) volume 29 of the *Code of Federal Regulations* as section 102.3.

_____

_____

_____

SECONDARY SOURCES

1. "Academic Legal Writing," a book by Eugene Volokh, published as a fourth edition in 2010 in New York by Foundation Press, which also published the first edition. You wish to cite to information on page 147 through 149 on cite-checking.

_____

_____

_____

2. An article entitled "Reputation Nation: Law in an Era of Ubiquitous Personal Information," by Lior Strahilevitz, published in volume 102 of the Northwestern University Law Review, beginning on page 1667, in 2008.

_____

_____

_____

3. Anna Karenina, a novel written by Leo Tolstoy in 1877 and originally published in that year. You are citing to the 1995 edition published in Oxford by Oxford University Press, which is not the original publisher. In this edition, the original text was translated by Louise Maude and Aylmer Maude.

_____

_____

_____

4. An article appearing on page 16, section A, in the May 7, 1999, edition of the *Wall Street Journal* entitled "Enron Gets $1.9 Billion Funding for India Plant." The authors of the article are Jonathan Karp and Kathryn Kranhold.

_____

_____

_____

5. An article by Paul D. Carrington entitled "Incorrect Speech, Incorrect Hearing: A Problem of Postmodern Legal Education." This article was published in 2003 in volume 53 of the Journal of Legal Education on page 404.

_____

_____

_____

6. The poem "Her Whole Life Is an Epigram" by William Blake, published in a 1994 collection entitled "William Blake" by the Oxford University Press in Oxford. The editor of the collection is Michael Mann. The poem appears on page 115.

_____

_____

_____

7. An unpublished working paper entitled "Policing Gun Crime Without Guns" by Tracey L. Meares and Andrew V. Papachristos, available on SSRN (the Social Science Research Network) at http://ssrn.com/abstract'1326932. It was completed and uploaded to that database on January 13, 2009, but it was not assigned a working paper number. You would like to cite to something on page 7.

_____

_____

_____

8. An article by Jacob Weisberg entitled "The Top 25 Bushisms of All Time," posted on the web magazine site *Slate* on January 12, 2009 and available at www.slate.com/id/2208132.

_____

_____

_____

9. "When Justice Lets Us Down," an article by Jim Dwyer, Peter Neufeld and Barry Scheck, published in the February 14, 2000, issue of the magazine *Newsweek*. The article appears on page 59. The authors' names are not particularly relevant to the point you are making.

_____

_____

_____

10. A comment posted by Gordon Smith to an original posting called "Law School Grading" on the blog *The Conglomerate*. Smith posted his comment on September 28, 2008. His comment and the original posting can be found at http://www.theconglomerate.org/2008/09/law-school-grad.html. This blog does not publish the time stamps of its postings.

_____

_____

SHORT FORMS

1. In the introduction of your case comment, you mentioned a book by Kent Greenawalt and provided a citation in your eighth footnote: KENT GREENAWALT, SPEECH, CRIME AND THE USE OF LANGUAGE (1989). Now, in the third section of your article, you wish to create a citation for use in a footnote that refers to page 103 of this book.

_____

_____

_____

2. A few sentences earlier, you mentioned a law review article by Douglas A. Kysar and provided a citation in your one hundred twenty-third footnote: Douglas A. Kysar, *The Expectations of Consumers*, 103 Colum. L. Rev. 1700 (2003). Now, after several intervening cites, you wish to create a citation for use in your one hundred thirtieth footnote that refers to page 1738 of this article.

_____

_____

3. In your article you will be referring to several articles by Lucinda M. Finley. The first article was published in 1998 and is entitled "The Hidden Victims of Tort Reform: Women, Children, and the Elderly." It appears in volume 53 of the Emory Law Journal, beginning on page 1263. You know that you will be citing this article numerous times, as well as other articles by Professor Finley. To distinguish this article from the others, you want to refer to it as "Hidden Victims." Create a first citation for this article, including a hereinafter nickname, for use in your footnote twenty-four.

_____

_____

_____

4. In a later footnote, you wish to refer back to the Finley article in your footnote twenty-four and direct your reader to pages 1270 through 1272. [For your reference, the text of Problem 3 is: In your article you will be referring to several articles by Lucinda M. Finley. The first article was published in 1998 and is entitled "The Hidden Victims of Tort Reform: Women, Children, and the Elderly." It appears in volume 53 of the Emory Law Journal, beginning on page 1263. You know that you will be citing this article numerous times, as well as other articles by Professor Finley. To distinguish this article from the others, you want to refer to it as "Hidden Victims." Create a first citation for this article, including a hereinafter nickname, for use in your footnote twenty-four.]

_____

_____

_____

5. In your fifteenth footnote, you created a citation to a famous case from the Court of Appeals of New York, *Palsgraf v. Long Island Railroad Company*, which appeared in volume 162 of the *Northeastern Reporter*, page 99, in 1928. You next want to cite to page 100 of this case in your thirtieth footnote. Create the appropriate citation for your footnote.

_____

_____

_____

6. In the next footnote, footnote thirty-one, you wish to cite to page 100 of *Palsgraf* again. Footnote thirty has only one citation within it. [For your reference, the text of Problem 5 is: In your fifteenth footnote, you created a citation to a famous case from the Court of Appeals of New York, *Palsgraf v. Long Island Railroad Company*, which appeared in volume 162 of the *Northeastern Reporter*, page 99, in 1928. You next want to cite to page 100 of this case in your thirtieth footnote. Create the appropriate citation for your footnote.]

_____

_____

_____

7. In footnote thirty-three, after several citations to *Overseas Tankership (U.K.) Ltd.*, you wish to cite *Palsgraf* again, this time to material on page 101. Create the citation. [For your reference, the text of Problem 5 is: In your fifteenth footnote, you created a citation to a famous case from the Court of Appeals of New York, *Palsgraf v. Long Island Railroad Company*, which appeared in volume 162 of the *Northeastern Reporter*, page 99, in 1928. You next want to cite to page 100 of this case in your thirtieth footnote. Create the appropriate citation for your footnote.]

_____

_____

_____

8. A few pages earlier in your academic article, you cited a Colorado statute, section 13-21-403, from the West code, published in a main volume in 2005. Now, after many intervening cites and twelve footnotes, you wish to cite the statute section again. Create the later citation.

_____

_____

_____

9. Two footnotes later, after citing two cases, you wish to cite this Colorado provision again. Create the later citation. [For your reference, the text of Problem 8 is: A few pages earlier in your academic article, you cited a Colorado statute, section 13-21-403, from the West code, published in a main volume in 2005. Now, after many intervening cites and twelve footnotes, you wish to cite the statute section again. Create the later citation.]

_____

_____

_____

10. In the second section of your seminar paper, you wish to cite a report entitled "Educating Lawyers: Preparation for the Profession of Law" that was authored and published by the Carnegie Foundation for the Advancement of Teaching in 2007. Five editors are listed, but you would like to save space by not listing all of them: William M. Sullivan, Anne Colby, Judith Welch Wegner, Lloyd Bond and Lee S. Shulman. You will be citing this report numerous times and will refer to it in text as the "Carnegie Report." Create a first citation for your forty-first footnote, including a hereinafter nickname that will be less cumbersome for later cross-references than the usual author-based cross-reference form would be.

_____

_____

_____

11. In footnote fifty, you wish to cite the Carnegie Report again, this time directing your reader to page 25. Create the citation. [For your reference, the text of Problem 10 is: In the second section of your seminar paper, you wish to cite to a report entitled "Educating Lawyers: Preparation for the Profession of Law" that was compiled and published by the Carnegie Foundation for the Advancement of Teaching in 2007. Five editors are listed: William M. Sullivan, Anne Colby, Judith Welch Wegner, Lloyd Bond and Lee S. Shulman. You will be citing to this report numerous times and refer to it in text as the "Carnegie Report." Create a first citation for your forty-first footnote, including a hereinafter nickname that will be less cumbersome for later cross-references than the usual author-based cross-reference form would be.]

_____

_____

_____

12. In the introduction to your seminar paper, you wish to give an overview of your paper's thesis and analysis. In doing so, you make the assertion that the Socratic method has never been empirically tested to be a superior form of information delivery than other classroom methods. You realize that this assertion needs support and therefore want to direct your reader to the fuller discussion of this assertion in Part IV of your paper. Create the citation for a footnote to this controversial assertion about the Socratic method using the signal "*see*."

_____

_____

_____

13. On second thought, you decide that you really want to direct your reader to particular authorities that appear in footnotes in Part IV, specifically in footnotes 80-92. These footnotes contain citation sentences, but no textual sentences. Create this citation, using the signal "*see*."

_____

_____

_____

14. Earlier in your article, in footnote 14, you cited a book written by Sandra M. Gilbert and Susan Gubar in 1979, entitled "The Madwoman in the Attic." Now, after many intervening cites, you wish to cite to pages 40 through 43 of that book in footnote 78. Create that later citation.

_____

_____

_____

15. Earlier in your article, in footnote fifty-two, you cited an obscenity case, *Miller v. California*, which was decided by the United States Supreme Court in 1973 and appears in volume 413 of *United States Reports*, page 15. Now, in footnote sixty-one, you would like to refer to page 36 of that decision.

_____

_____

_____

16. In footnote sixty-two, with no intervening cite, you would like to refer to page 24 of the *Miller* decision. Footnote sixty-one contains only one citation. [For your reference, the text of Problem 15 is: Earlier in your article, in footnote fifty-two, you cited an obscenity case, *Miller v. California*, which was decided by the United States Supreme Court in 1973 and appears in volume 413 of *United States Reports*, page 15. Now, in footnote sixty-one, you would like to refer to page 36 of that decision.]

_____

_____

_____

17. In footnote sixty-five, after cites to other obscenity cases, you wish to cite to page 24 of *Miller* again. [For your reference, the text of Problem 15 is: Earlier in your article, in footnote fifty-two, you cited an obscenity case, *Miller v. California*, which was decided by the United States Supreme Court in 1973 and appears in volume 413 of *United States Reports*, page 15. Now, in footnote sixty-one, you would like to refer to page 36 of that decision.]

_____

_____

_____

18. You wish to cite to an amicus curiae (friend of court) brief called "Brief for Women's Legal Defense Fund as Amici Curiae Supporting Respondents." The brief was filed in support of the U.S. government's position in *United States v. Foster*, 598 A.2d 724 (D.C. 1981). The docket number of the case is 80-1034. You would like to create a citation to this brief and also create a nickname for this source. You refer to the brief as "WLDF Brief" in text.

---

19. A few footnotes back, in footnote seventy-one, you created a citation for an article that appeared in the January 4, 2009 edition of the *New York Times* on page 2 of Section E, entitled "The Tightrope of Managing a Law Office," by Anita J. Cicero. Now, in footnote seventy-eight, you would like to cite this article again.

---

20. You wish to cite again in footnote one hundred twelve a book that you cited in footnote ninety-seven of your seminar paper, Niall Ferguson's 2008 book, "The Ascent of Money." You wish to refer to page 33 of the book. Create the citation for footnote one hundred twelve.